THE FOUNTAINHEAD

An American Novel

TWAYNE'S MASTERWORK STUDIES

Robert Lecker, General Editor

THE FOUNTAINHEAD

An American Novel

Douglas J. Den Uyl

TWAYNE PUBLISHERS
New York

Twayne's Masterwork Studies No. 169

The Fountainhead: An American Novel
Douglas J. Den Uyl

Twayne Publishers
1633 Broadway
New York, NY 10019

Library of Congress Cataloging-in-Publication Data

Den Uyl, Douglas J., 1950–
    The fountainhead : an American novel / Douglas J. Den Uyl.
       p.   cm. — (Twayne's masterwork studies ; no. 169)
    Includes bibliographical references (p.   ) and index.
    ISBN 0-8057-7932-9 (alk. paper)
    1. Rand, Ayn. Fountainhead. 2. Didactic fiction, American—
History and criticism.   3. Individualism in literature.
    4. Philosophy in literature.   5. Ethics in literature.   I. Title.
II. Series.
PS3535.A547F6934   1999
813'.52—dc21   98-49012
                                                 CIP

Contents

Note on the References and Acknowledgments

The edition of *The Fountainhead* referred to throughout this work is the 25th-anniversary hardbound edition published by Bobbs-Merrill in 1968. With an author as popular and recent as Ayn Rand, there is little problem in finding copies of *The Fountainhead,* and there are no special concerns about the text (e.g., concerns about translations or textual changes between editions). The work is available in virtually any bookstore in an inexpensive paperback edition. Hardbound copies are readily available as well.

A number of people were very helpful to me during the writing of this manuscript: Douglas Rasmussen, Tibor Machan, Chris Sciabarra, Mimi Gladstein, Eric Mack, Elizabeth A. Miller, Louis Torres and Michelle Kamhi, Stuart Warner, Chandran Kukathas, Barbara Branden, and Rosalind Parnes of the Bellarmine College library. Eric Mack, Stuart Warner, and Tibor Machan deserve special thanks for looking over drafts of the interpretation portion of the manuscript and making numerous useful suggestions. Finally, Douglas Rasmussen not only commented on many versions of the entire manuscript but at one point saved it from the depths of cyberspace. For his help and friendship, particularly with respect to our years of thinking about Ayn Rand, a "thank you" is hardly sufficient.

What follows is a work of interpretation. The views I express should not necessarily be attached to anyone just named.

Chronology: Ayn Rand's Life and Works

1905	Born Alissa Zinovievna Rosenbaum in St. Petersburg, Russia, on February 2. Her parents, Fronz and Anna, are upper middle class and of Jewish decent.
1914	Alissa is writing her own stories and reads a French story, "The Mysterious Valley," by Maurice Champange. The hero Cyrus is the prototype for many of Rand's later heroes, such as Roark and Rearden. The name Kira from *We the Living* is the feminine of Cyrus.
	Russia is at war with Germany and Austria (World War I).
1917–1918	The Russian Revolution takes place; the Rosenbaum family, in a precarious position, moves to the Crimea.
1921	Alissa graduates from high school; the Crimea falls permanently to the Reds; Alissa burns her diary in fear that her ideas might mean imprisonment for her or her family.
1921–1922	Alissa attends the University of Petrograd and studies ancient philosophy under N. O. Losky; she reads Nietzsche and has her first serious love interest.
1924	Graduates from the University of Petrograd with highest honors.
1926	Travels to the United States and adopts the name Ayn Rand. She lives in Chicago with relatives for a while but moves to Los Angeles. She begins work for Cecil B. DeMille and meets her future husband, Frank O'Connor.
1930	Begins working on *We the Living,* her first novel.
1932	Writes original screenplay *Red Pawn,* which is purchased by Universal, then Paramount, but never produced.
1933	Completes *We the Living* and sells *Penthouse Legend,* a play.
1934	*Penthouse Legend* opens at the Hollywood Playhouse under the title *Woman on Trial.* The play is sold for production on Broadway. Rand writes the novelette *Ideal,* which she later turned into a play. It was not produced until 1984, after her death.

1935	*Penthouse Legend* opens as *Night of January 16th.*
1936	*We the Living* is published a month after the closing of a successful run of *Night of January 16th.* Rand begins work on *The Fountainhead.*
1937	Writes *Anthem* but is unable to sell it to American publishers. It is sold to the British publisher of *We the Living* in 1938.
1938–1940	Writes the play *Think Twice* but is unable to sell it. The play version of *We the Living,* entitled *Unconquered,* is produced and opens in February of 1940 but is unsuccessful.
1940	Joins the Willkie presidential campaign to help defeat the collectivist tendencies of Roosevelt. She becomes disillusioned with Willkie but meets a number of "conservative" thinkers of the day: Ruth Alexander, Albert J. Nock, Rose Wilder Lane, and Isabel Paterson.
1941	Connects with Archibald G. Ogden, who, after seeing some early chapters, stakes his career at Bobbs-Merrill on *The Fountainhead.* She signs a contract for the book in December with the completion deadline of January 1, 1943.
1943	*The Fountainhead* is published in May. Early sales are sluggish, but controversy over the book begins anyway. Rand sells the movie rights to *The Fountainhead* and returns to California to live.
1944–1949	Works for Hal Wallis in Hollywood (who produces the movie version of *The Fountainhead*) and begins writing *Atlas Shrugged.* She testifies before the House Un-American Activities Committee in 1947. The movie version of *The Fountainhead* is released in 1949.
1950–1957	Befriends psychologist Nathaniel Branden in 1950. She continues working on *Atlas Shrugged* and talks to numerous publishers but selects Random House. She finishes the book in March 1957; it is published in October.
1958	Founding of NBI (Nathaniel Branden Institute), devoted to explaining and advancing Rand's philosophical ideas.
1960	Rand delivers her first talk at a university (Yale). She receives many other invitations afterward.
1963–1964	Receives an honorary degree of Doctor of Humane Letters from Lewis and Clark College. Both major novels are selling well. She does a famous interview with *Playboy* magazine in March of 1964 and gives the first of her Ford Hall Forum lectures in Boston, which became an annual tradition.
1968	NBI is dismantled.
1964–1971	Rand begins writing nonfiction works seriously, starting with the *Objectivist Newsletter* in 1964. The books she produces during this period are *The Virtue of Selfishness* (1964), *Capi-*

talism: The Unknown Ideal (1966), *The Romantic Manifesto* (1971), and *The New Left: The Anti-Industrial Revolution* (1971).

1971–1981   Makes few public appearances and writes little except for the *Ayn Rand Letter* (discontinued in 1975). Frank O'Connor dies in 1979. Rand gives her last talk to the National Committee for Monetary Reform in November of 1981.

1982   Ayn Rand dies March 6. *Philosophy: Who Needs It* is published posthumously.

LITERARY AND
HISTORICAL CONTEXT

1

Historical Context

Between 1905, the year of Ayn Rand's birth, and 1945, shortly after *The Fountainhead* was published, the most significant political and social events of the twentieth century took place. These events include two world wars, a great economic depression, the dropping of the first atomic bomb, and the reigns of Joseph Stalin and Adolf Hitler. Many of the events of this era were spearheaded by anti-individualist collectivist ideologies such as socialism and communism. *The Fountainhead* is a book about the meaning and importance of the individual.

Nineteen fourteen marked the beginning of World War I. A year earlier the United States had established the legal beginning of its later plunge into welfare statism with a constitutional amendment permitting the progressive income tax. But Ayn Rand was born in Russia, where many significant changes were taking place that would affect both her native land and the world at large. On the heels of civil war due to Russian military failures during World War I and due to corruption in the czarist court, the Bolshevik revolution began in 1917. Rand's family was bourgeois and thus part of the class vilified by the newly installed Communist government. Lenin, for example, began his rule of communist Russia by confiscating all private lands. The ideology proclaimed that people were no longer allowed to live for their own private, "selfish" interests but must look to the collective good, usually interpreted to mean the good of the proletariat or working class. In 1926, the year Ayn Rand left for America, Stalin exiled Trotsky, and by 1929 Stalin was in complete control of the Union of Soviet Socialist Republics (USSR).

The first two decades of the twentieth century also saw the rise of "progressive" movements throughout the West. In the United States, for example, the Progressive Party, which supported government ownership of utilities and advocated "pro labor" legislation, was formed. Though the White House was dominated by Republican presidents, including Calvin Coolidge, during the 1920s (with the exception of the progressive Woodrow Wilson at the opening of the decade), the Progressive Party—and progressivism in general—had the sympathy of most intellectuals and socialists.

Elsewhere in the world more militant forms of socialism were developing. In Germany the National Socialist German Worker's Party elected Adolf Hitler as its "unlimited chairman" in 1921. Though it would be many years before Hitler took complete control of Germany, National Socialism in the meantime competed with other forms of socialism and communism for political control. So-called liberal ideologies—those sympathetic to economic and political liberty—were steadily losing political influence. Financial and economic problems in Germany, as elsewhere, undoubtedly contributed to an atmosphere conducive to socialist and communist appeal. These ideologies claimed there was a connection between the problems in society and capitalism and were presented as the alternative wave of the future.

The 1930s saw not only the dictatorships of Stalin and Hitler but also America's Great Depression and the beginning of the New Deal. Government increased its involvement in managing society and in regulating the lives of individuals. There was hardly an area, from housing and retirement to employment practices, in which the government was not present. Though Franklin Roosevelt ran on a free-market platform in 1932, he had firmly established the welfare state in the United States by the end of the decade. As Roosevelt put it, the state would guarantee "a proper security, a reasonable leisure, and a decent living throughout life" for all its citizens.[1] By this time, Rand was becoming politically active, and she campaigned against Roosevelt in the 1940 election. Though disillusioned when Roosevelt won the election, she began to form connections with various conservative thinkers of that period.[2]

In September of 1939 Germany invaded Poland and began World War II. The United States officially entered the war after the Japanese bombed Pearl Harbor in 1941. It is remarkable that although Rand considered collectivism one of the root causes of this war, neither she nor her critics often mentioned the war in her work. *The Fountainhead* was completed and published during these war years, and yet one would have little sense of it from either this work or her letters of the period. Perhaps this is because war, though the quintessential collective effort in practice, was for Rand the *result* of certain principles rather than a statement of them. Perhaps it is because Rand herself could not fight or because her husband was too old for the military. Perhaps Rand, like some conservatives of that era, was ambivalent about, or opposed to, the United States' entry into the war. Maybe all the foregoing are reasons. Whatever the explanation, one of the most significant events of the first half of the twentieth century goes largely unmentioned in Rand's work.

It would be a mistake, however, to conclude that war had no impact on Rand. As she was to say much later in her essay "The Roots of War": "[S]tatism *needs* war; a free country does not. . . . Germany and Russia needed war; the United States did not and gained nothing"(37). For Rand, war, perhaps especially World War II, was an example of what happens when one looks to the state rather than to trade and cooperation among individuals as the means to social order, prosperity, and peaceful coexistence.

> Let those who are actually concerned with peace observe that *capitalism gave mankind the longest period of peace in history*—a period during which there were no wars involving the entire civilized world—from the end of the Napoleonic wars in 1815 to the outbreak of World War I in 1914. (38; my emphasis)

World War II, then, may have been for Rand one of the most dramatic symbols of the problem with statism and collectivism, despite the war's infrequent mention in her work.

THE LITERARY CONTEXT

This era also produced some well-known novelists. Sinclair Lewis, Gertrude Stein (whom Rand satirizes in *The Fountainhead*),[4] F. Scott Fitzgerald, John Steinbeck, John Dos Passos, Zora Neale Hurston, and James T. Farrell, for example, all wrote in the this period, as did Ernest Hemingway, William Faulkner, and Thomas Wolfe. A number of these authors did not paint a pleasing picture of the United States and its institutions, and social criticism was a common element in so-called serious literature. Either explicitly or tacitly, individualism, capitalism, business, or American culture generally are disparaged in a number of the writings of this period. Rand—though often no less critical than other authors of what she found around her—did not resolve her criticisms into such collectivist concepts as the "working class," the "common good," or the "welfare of the community." Rather, she believed in an individualism that manifests itself in independent judgment and productive work. Rand holds up the United States as being grounded in essentially the right principles. In contrast to a number of other authors, consequently, she comes across as very pro-American. Indeed, Rand stands so alone in her values, style, and sensibilities that she is seldom mentioned in discussions of important authors prior to 1950. Part of the reason for this exclusion is that her later novel *Atlas Shrugged* often overshadows *The Fountainhead*, but another part is certainly that Rand saw herself as opposing many of the values being portrayed in the literature and art of her era.

In light of the events and circumstances of the first half of the twentieth century, it can be said that collectivism—whether of a mild "social democratic" variety or a more militant form of communism and socialism—was everywhere on the rise. In rhetoric about the "working class," "humanity," the "common good," and the "public interest," which intellectuals, artists, and the popular press espoused, the climate of this period—and undoubtedly afterward as well—was largely devoid of individualist sentiments. Undoubtedly, judging from the sales, *The Fountainhead* gave voice to values that were latent in many people but had not found expression. Rand describes her success with *The Fountainhead* as follows: "It was as if an underground stream flowed through the country and broke out in sudden springs that shot to the surface at random, in unpredictable places."[5] The novel is a powerful and compelling statement of individualist values in its own right, but it gains even more impact by being so opposed to the sensibilities of its era.

RAND'S LIFE

In most respects Rand's life was as unconventional as her novels; in other respects great bulks of it were spent simply writing. Our purpose here is not to pretend to an abbreviated biography. Rather, our purpose is to highlight briefly some facets of Ayn Rand's life that may be significant in understanding her fiction.

Ayn Rand was born Alissa Rosenbaum on February 2, 1905, in St. Petersburg, Russia.[6] Her parents were well situated and her early childhood normal. Alice was precocious and gifted and began inventing stories and characters at an early age. At nine she read a story, "The Mysterious Valley,"[7] whose hero, Cyrus, made a deep and lasting impression on her. The story is a romantic adventure story in which good is pitted against evil, and Cyrus rescues a beautiful girl in the end. Barbara Branden quotes Rand talking about Cyrus:

> "One illustration that particularly impressed me was a picture of Cyrus standing with a sword. He was a perfect drawing of my present hero: tall, long-legged, with leggings but no jacket, just an open collar, his shirt torn in front, open very low, sleeves rolled to the elbows, and hair falling down over one eye. The appearance of my heroes, and what is *my* type of man, was completely taken from that illustration."

The relatively idyllic quality of Rand's childhood ended with the coming of the Russian Revolution. This was also a time when Rand gained her first sense of political ideology. She was moved by Alexander Kerensky and his language of individual freedom, and she was opposed to communism. Her reasons for opposing communism—that it meant one must live for the state rather than for one's own purposes—remained unchanged throughout her life.

Rand's family fortunes diminished considerably after the Bolshevik factions of the revolution succeeded in gaining power. Nevertheless, Rand obtained a free university education and during that period had her first exposure to America through films. America seemed to her a land of active, purposeful people enjoying the fruits of freedom. Though Rand would later make many critical comments about America, she never wavered from the belief that her earliest image really did describe America's essential nature.

But the movies also had another significant place in Rand's life. After she was able to escape her native land and come to the United States at the age of 21, Rand managed to obtain work in the movie business in Hollywood, first as an extra and finally as a screenwriter. She began working for Cecil B. DeMille. It is difficult to know exactly what influence Hollywood had on Rand. She met her husband, Frank O'Connor, there. Her novels sometimes have the pace and dialogue structure of a Hollywood film of the '30s or '40s. She sold scripts to Hollywood, some of which were produced, some not, and when *The Fountainhead* was made into a film, she wrote the script. Rumors of *Atlas Shrugged* being made into a movie circulated into the latter years of Rand's life. In addition, Rand opposed many of the leftist and communist tendencies in Hollywood and testified before the House Un-American Activities Committee in the late 1940s. In some respects, then, it seems safe to claim that Hollywood was always a part of Rand's adult life. Though she formed her ideas on plot and on the battle between good and evil before entering Hollywood, Hollywood nevertheless had an enormous influence, even if its exact impact is difficult to isolate and specify.

It was during her university years in Russia that Rand took up the formal study of philosophy. She studied under the well-known professor N. O. Lossky and gained her first appreciation of Aristotle from him. Nevertheless, Rand was dissatisfied with both academic philosophy and Russian literature courses and ended up majoring in history (though she minored in philosophy). There are undoubtedly a number of interesting avenues to explore in considering Rand's education and its possible influence on her ideas, but pursuing them would take us too far afield.[8] What seems evident overall is that Rand was a person of definite opinions who easily and quickly assessed the worth of ideas as she confronted them. History seemed to her the most factual of the disciplines in the humanities, which fits well with her reality-based philosophy. Given Rand's later development of her own philosophy, it is evident that philosophy would have interested her to some degree. But Rand understood philosophy in a very special way, namely as a means to clarifying and objectifying one's thought. This understanding may not be the only or even the central understanding of philosophy as it is historically found in Western intellectual tradition.

It is not out of line to think of Rand's life during the '30s and '40s as being much like her depiction of Howard Roark's life. One can imagine her spending most of her days from early morning to late evening poring over her manuscripts, much as Roark would be occupied with his designs. Like Roark's, her professional work was punctuated with long periods when she had to work at anything she could find. She was able to sell some of her work, including the successful *Night of January 16th,* but for the most part money was tight prior to the publication of *The Fountainhead.* Like Roark, Rand was an outsider, though she was perhaps not as vilified prior to the publication of *Atlas Shrugged* as Roark often was as an architect. In general, what one learns from this period, and what is true through most of Rand's life, is her incredible ability to focus and her extreme dedication to her work. All Rand's leading heroic characters are like her in this respect.

From the time of the Russian Revolution to the end of her life, Rand was passionately interested in politics. From the '30s into the '60s, Rand socialized or was acquainted with some of the leading conservative intellectuals of the day—people such as Isabel Paterson, Henry and Frances Hazlitt, and Ludwig and Margit von Mises. In all cases, there was eventually friction or a falling out. Perhaps Rand's sometimes volatile personality and the uniqueness of her ideas, not to mention her intransigent advocacy of them, conspired to make settledness in friendships of ideas unlikely. Political concepts can be controversial enough without the added dimensions of a strong will and a unique doctrine. But it must also be noted that Rand was never really at home among most conservatives.

The publication of *Atlas Shrugged* not only put Ayn Rand on the map as a controversial political thinker, but it forever divided her from the conservative movement. Beginning with the vituperative review of *Atlas Shrugged* by Whittaker Chambers in the *National Review*[9]—the leading voice of American conservatism at the time—Rand and conservatism were often at odds. The antipathy largely resulted from Rand's conviction that conservatives were disinclined firmly to separate church and state, but there are other differences as well. Perhaps those differences can be summed up by saying that Rand had little use for tradition and custom as arguments for principles of social order, and she celebrated reason rather than touted its limitations. Moreover, Rand was not particularly conservative with respect to other issues of importance to conservatives, such as sexuality and family.

In the 1960s, in part due to Rand's influence, conservatism split in two, with one part retaining the word *conservative* and the other adopting the term *libertarian*. Libertarians are more radically free-market–oriented than conservatives and more antistatist. They also tend to be more liberal on social issues such as drug control and abortion. Although Rand resisted being linked to libertarianism, especially the Libertarian Party, her name today has become closely allied with its principles.

Ayn Rand labeled her philosophy Objectivism, and during the late 1950s and 1960s her protégés Nathaniel and Barbara Branden began promoting her ideas through the Nathaniel Branden Institute, or NBI. Since questions were pouring in from readers about her philosophy, the institute offered courses and lectures on Rand's ideas. A newsletter and then a small magazine containing delineations of Objectivist concepts, social commentary, and book and movie reviews, as well as a mail-order book service, were established. During these years Rand wrote some of her most significant nonfiction works, which dealt with everything from abstract philosophy (e.g., *The Virtue of Selfishness*) to politics (e.g., *Capitalism: The Unknown Ideal*). It was also during this period that Rand had a love affair with Nathaniel Branden with the "consent" of their respective spouses. That affair eventually broke the Brandens up, destroyed NBI, and created an irrevocable schism in the movement, remnants of which exist to this day. During the 1970s Rand published more nonfiction and continued to be identified with libertarian causes, though that movement was beginning to spawn other leaders as well. The excitement and purposefulness of the NBI years, however, was gone forever.

Today those who were once students, followers, or dedicated admirers of Ayn Rand are successful in a wide variety of professions and occupations. Some, such as Alan Greenspan, have gained national prominence. Many have gone on to teach in colleges and universities. There is an Ayn Rand society that meets regularly in conjunction with the American Philosophical Association. Books continue to be published about Rand's philosophy, and Rand's own works still sell briskly. In recent years there has been a particularly strong renewal of interest in Ayn Rand and her works. Perhaps no other name is more widely associated with individualism, capitalism, and libertarianism than hers.

Yet in saying these things about Rand's influence we have moved from the context that surrounds her novels to their impact on our culture. Rand is an interesting author precisely because the cultural context in which we, the reader, confront her novels has been partly shaped by the novels themselves. Furthermore, the context in which the author wrote is not so distant from us in time, or so foreign to us in nature, that we are unfamiliar with it, as might be said of an author who wrote centuries ago. This is a benefit in approaching the novels, but it can also be a problem in appreciating them, for there is always the danger that we will reduce the works to familiar categories.

Rand herself was concerned about an aspect of this last issue. She had an ambivalence, to say the least, toward the whole idea of the relevance of historical context to her work. Rand believed that the intellectual influences on her were very limited, that her novels transcended history and spoke to the ages, and that the values she espoused should be judged on their own merits and not in light of their historical setting. Some recent scholars have begun to consider Rand's historical context more systematically,[10] but she herself would likely have resisted the notion that she could be better understood by such investigations. Still, it is hard to imagine that Rand would deny that the rising collectivist sentiments of her era had something to do with the themes of her novels and the way she wrote them. Moreover, however independent one may think oneself, there is always the possibility of unacknowledged or unrecognized influences that are worth investigation by those interested in an author's life and work. Nevertheless, Rand wanted her work to have a certain timeless quality, and she believed that fundamental principles and values transcended circumstances and historical epochs. Truth was objective for her, and in this sense she was very much opposed to the historicist tendencies of recent times in both literature and philosophy.

2

The Importance of the Work

One of the central problems in discussing the importance of *The Fountainhead* is moving it out from under the shadow of Rand's magnum opus, *Atlas Shrugged,* and from Rand's later nonfiction writing and reputation. It is not that *The Fountainhead* should be divorced from these other aspects of Rand's life and writings but rather that our understanding of the importance of this novel is difficult to measure in its own right. In addition, Rand encourages the view that her work is a seamless whole, and her critics and admirers alike have supported that claim. The problem with viewing Rand's work as a seamless whole is that doing so makes it virtually impossible to give any special importance to only one piece of the whole, such as *The Fountainhead.* In this respect, then, we might just concede that *The Fountainhead* has no special importance with respect to the entire phenomenon of Ayn Rand. This book, in other words, *is* no different from others in representing many of the ideas (e.g., egoism, capitalism, individualism, atheism, libertarianism, rationalism) that made Rand the intriguing and controversial thinker that she was.

Another way of tackling our problem is simply to ignore the Ayn Rand who existed after 1945 and examine the importance of *The*

Fountainhead in terms of its own period. There is value to this approach, but in many respects we considered the problem this way in the last chapter. We noted there that Rand gave voice to values like individualism that were not then getting expression elsewhere in the literary, artistic, or political world. We need add here only that it is not merely the *expression* of certain values that gives *The Fountainhead* its importance for the period, but the unique and profound way in which Rand defends those values. Individualism is not defended as being good, for example, because it is the basis for capitalism and capitalism will make us wealthier or better off. Rather, for Rand the benefits we derive from capitalism are the consequence of living according to the sorts of principles that are good for (that is, suited to) human life. Individualism, in other words, is the good, and the beneficial consequences are derived from it rather than the reverse. Indeed, Rand's individualism goes well beyond any previous defense, for the individual is the *ultimate* value for Rand—not the state, or society, or God, or the community, or the economy, or any other collective or transcendent ideal. Rand's defense of individualism is therefore both new and radical, and in this respect *The Fountainhead* may be the first statement of such a foundational notion of individualism. Add to this the emotional power of the novel, and one can see its importance for the period, if not afterward.

Nevertheless, it might plausibly be argued that the presentation of individualism and other values in *The Fountainhead* is overpowered by the even more extended treatment of them in *Atlas Shrugged*. We might ask, then, why one might recommend *The Fountainhead* over *Atlas Shrugged*. Ignoring reasons such as *The Fountainhead* is a less daunting treatment of its themes than *Atlas Shrugged,* and granting that *Atlas Shrugged* is the more necessary of the two in understanding Ayn Rand's overall thought, is it possible to say anything about *The Fountainhead* that recommends it in its own right over *Atlas Shrugged*?

Following up on some hints made in the last chapter, it can be argued that *The Fountainhead* is the quintessential presentation of American individualism, American optimism, and the promise that is America. *Atlas Shrugged*, by contrast, rises out of the ashes of America. In depicting a new social order it bears a certain utopian quality that looks at America from the outside. *The Fountainhead,* on the other hand, takes its bearings from *within* the American context. It does not offer a blueprint for restructuring all of society but rather calls American society to its own inherent principles. Howard Roark does not speak to us at the end as John Galt does at the end of *Atlas Shrugged*—from the outside. Roark gives an account of what he stands for within an established institutional setting of a particular culture—that is, from within an American courtroom. He defends American individualism. In this way *The Fountainhead* carries forward at least one type of reading of the individualist understanding of America.

The individualist understanding of America has been with us for a long time. Consider, for example, this statement of America presented in 1782:

> The American ought therefore to love this country much better than that wherein either he or his forefathers were born. Here the rewards of his industry follow with equal steps the progress of his labour; his labour is founded on the basis of nature, *self-interest;* can it want a stronger allurement? Wives and children, who before in vain demanded of him a morsel of bread, now, fat and frolicsome, gladly help their father to clear those fields whence exuberant crops are to arise to feed and to clothe them all; without any part being claimed, either by a despotic prince, a rich abbot, or a mighty lord.[1]

Notice the individualistic elements described in this passage. We reap the rewards of our own labor and are moved by our own goals and interests. No authority can tell us how to live or demand a share of our lives without our consent. Productivity is the central practical virtue, and all these values are in accord with the way human beings are meant to live. Happiness and abundance are the results of this way of life. Today, individualism might be expressed this way:

> I do not choose to be a common man.
> It is my right to be uncommon—if I can.
> I seek opportunity—not security. I do not wish to be a kept citizen, humbled and dulled by having the state look after me.

I want to take a calculated risk; to dream and to build, to fail and to succeed.

I refuse to barter incentive for a dole. I prefer the challenges of life to the guaranteed existence; the thrill of fulfillment to the stale calm of utopia.

I will not trade freedom for beneficence nor my dignity for a handout. I will never cower before any master nor bend to any threat.

It is my heritage to stand erect, proud and unafraid; to think and act for myself, enjoy the benefit of my creations and to face the world boldly and say, this I have done.

All this is what it means to be an American.[2]

Here again we have the values of productivity and independence, though framed by a suspicion of more modern forms of political authority (e.g., the "state" instead of the "lord"). But there is an argument here as well—one that is like Rand's own, namely that the *uncommon* rather than the common man defines more accurately what it means to be an American.

Individualism, then, is a long-standing part of the American consciousness. In this sense *The Fountainhead* is but another expression of that tradition, though it is both far deeper and more complex than the usual sentimentalist expressions in passages like the two just cited. *The Fountainhead* is arguably the best statement ever made of the American individualist tradition. Rand's critics might say it is best in the sense of glorifying individualism above and to the exclusion of all else. Rand's admirers would argue that it is best because it captures the true nature of individualism in a way never before clarified and presents that view in a powerful and compelling statement. At a minimum I believe we can agree that *The Fountainhead* is a unique presentation of the meaning of individualism. More important, it is a statement of the meaning of *American* individualism unlike any other work by Ayn Rand. The values Howard Roark and Dominique Francon represent may transcend a particular culture, but these characters' representation of their values as the essence of that culture does not.

3

Critical Reception

The Fountainhead is a remarkable book in many ways, but one of its most remarkable traits is the lack of critical attention it has received. This lack of attention is all the more amazing given that it is a bestseller and given Ayn Rand's controversial ideas. One would have expected a work like *The Fountainhead* to generate many reviews, however much in disagreement with the book's ideas a reviewer might be. Instead, one finds only a handful of reviews.

It is not that *The Fountainhead* lacked exposure in the right places when it came out. Rand's play *Night of January 16th* was a successful Broadway production by then, and Rand had no real reputation as a controversial thinker prior to *The Fountainhead.* Consequently, New York reviewers would have no previous prejudices toward Rand and should, in fact, have had an interest in someone who had been a successful playwright there. The *New York Times* did review the book in 1943 when it came out. The reviewer, Lorine Pruette, gave it a positive review and said of Rand that "she has a subtle and ingenious mind and the capacity of writing brilliantly, beautifully, bitterly."[1] The *Nation*—which described itself as a leading "liberal" magazine—also mentioned the book but signaled the future by giving it only one disparaging paragraph.[2] During the same period N. L. Rothman reviewed the book for the *Saturday Review,* saying the writing was "strong, dramatic, everywhere intense, and highly articulate." He even likened Rand to Sinclair Lewis.[3] But Rothman also accused Rand of a "confusion of values" when her rejection of collectivism led her to "conscienceless individualism." Most everyone at the time recommended the novel in some form, but there was no flurry of reviews or scholarly disquisitions on the book.

The passage of time, through which the book never lagged in popularity or sales, did little to increase critical attention. The 25th anniversary of the publication of *The Fountainhead* did generate a retrospective review in the *New York Times Book Review,*[4] but although the review conceded the power of the book, it also described the novel as "silly" and "better read when one is young enough to miss the point." By the time the book reached its 50th anniversary, it was virtually ignored by literary critics (except those who were followers of Rand[5]), though popularity and sales were still strong. The Lorine Pruette review was, however, included a few years after the 50th anniversary in a special edition of the *New York Times Book Review* that reprinted 70 significant reviews from the past.[6]

One might try to explain the lack of attention by suggesting that Rand is a "popular" rather than a "serious" writer. It is hard to imagine someone who convincingly regards Rand to be *merely* a popular novelist, given the length of her books and the philosophizing they contain. Rand herself never thought there had to be a divorce between popularity and substance. Not only are her novels some of the best-selling novels of all time but also they are often a part of coursework in high school and college classrooms. Perhaps Rand has been ignored by critics because she appeals to ideas that are popular, but not in vogue in intellectual circles. And given her disparagement of those circles, one might expect that she would be ignored, vilified, or scorned by people who fancy themselves intellectual or interested in "serious" literature. Yet speculation about Rand's lackluster attention from critics seems somewhat pointless, if for no other reason than that the explanations could be many. Moreover, she is a fairly recent author, and assessment of reactions to an artist within his or her own time is fraught with difficulties. We can say with some assurance, however, that although *The Fountainhead* has been relatively neglected, the person and phenomenon of Ayn Rand have not, and herein lies a now-familiar problem.

Separating what critics might think about *The Fountainhead* from the whole of Rand and her work is difficult. As we noted in the last chapter, this novel gets lumped with *Atlas Shrugged* as well as with Rand's idiosyncratic personality and radical politics. When one does get to comments about *The Fountainhead,* particularly by unsympathetic critics, they are often dismissive in tone rather than substantive in analysis. Barbara Harrison, for example, describes *The Fountainhead* as "a ripe and fanciful mixture of politics and sex" in which Rand sets up "straw figures for her heroes and heroines to knock down," the heroes and heroines themselves "given to the utterance of bromides."[7] She also mocks the novel for being overly dramatic—like a Hollywood movie of the '40s—as well as for its view of romance and women: "Rand gave women haughty, indomitable, fierce heroines—who sang in their chains and found ecstasy in surrender."[8]

RAND THE WRITER

Others are unfriendly to Rand's literary efforts because they believe she is a bad writer. A typical example of such criticism is as follows:

> For above all, Miss Rand is a horrendously bad writer. Her prose is a melange of bastard Hemingway and limping *Time*-style; her characters are so superficially and shallowly etched in that it is not even correct to label them pasteboard; and the dialogue she gives her characters is undifferentiated and monotonously overblown.[9]

Since Rand's style is rather similar in *The Fountainhead* and *Atlas Shrugged,* Robert White, in making these comments about her work generally, is also directing them specifically at *The Fountainhead* and gives examples to that effect.

Yet Rand as a writer is by no means without her defenders when it comes to *The Fountainhead*. Stephen Cox, for example, observes that "Rand's talents as a satirist, which are very considerable, have escaped the notice of almost everyone who has commented on her work."[10] Besides her skill as a satirist, Cox points to Rand's insights into American character types and her abilities as an aphorist. With respect to the latter, Cox offers a helpful example:

> One wonders how much impact *The Fountainhead* would retain if Roark had been made to observe that "thinking gets done inside the heads of individual people and not in consultative groups," etc., instead of announcing, aphoristically, that "there is no such thing as a collective brain." . . . The supposedly minor art of the aphorism is one tool that Rand uses to charge every part of her novel with the meaning of the whole.[11]

Other favorable commentators on Rand's literary work go so far as to say that "from a strictly literary perspective *The Fountainhead* is a better novel [than *Atlas Shrugged*]. Both extol the same individualistic virtues, but *The Fountainhead* does so in a more concise and unified manner."[12]

It is clear that Rand's writing is every bit as controversial as her ideas. One must in the end, of course, form one's own judgments. What is universally conceded, however, is that rather little attention has been paid to Rand as a literary artist. Her critics would claim she has gotten the attention she deserves in this area. Yet what must be recognized is that most independent critics have simply not made the effort to look at Rand's work with some real understanding of her philosophy or from within the framework of her own values and principles. There is much that could, and hopefully will, be done in this respect, as Rand's artistic endeavors gain increased attention in their own right.

CRITICAL RECEPTION IN GENERAL

As we have already noted, the phenomenon that is Ayn Rand is largely a result of the appearance of *Atlas Shrugged*. If Rand had written only

The Fountainhead, she might still hold some place as a notable twentieth-century novelist and thinker, but it is unlikely that she would be so well known and controversial. In discussing general issues associated with Rand's intellectual legacy, therefore, our problem is to find those topics that clearly arise with *The Fountainhead* and yet do not force us to read it simply through the eyes of *Atlas Shrugged.* Our intent, then, is to keep *The Fountainhead* as "clean" and unfettered with other sources as possible. Something, nevertheless, needs to be said about contemporary responses to themes that may have been given prominence as a result of *Atlas Shrugged,* but which nevertheless have a substantial foundation in *The Fountainhead.* Two such themes seem particularly compelling in this respect: individualism and feminism.

Beginning first with feminism, we shall see in a later chapter that Dominique may be the central character of *The Fountainhead.* Dagny Taggart is certainly the central character of *Atlas Shrugged.* In both books we find strong, independent female lead characters. These women are quite superior to the vast majority of men around them and every bit the equal of the best men in intelligence, career, and character. Indeed, as one might expect from a work of "romantic fiction" (a term explained more fully in the next chapter), the central female character in Rand's novels is superior to *all* men save the one she ends up with in the end. The pivotal place given to these women and their equality, if not superiority, to the best of men naturally raise the issue of Rand's connection to feminism. The issue also arises because Rand claimed that the essence of femininity is hero worship of a man![13]

Historically there has been little written on this topic, again perhaps because Rand stood outside the circles of academics and literati where such questions are routinely discussed. A noteworthy exception is Mimi Gladstein's article "Ayn Rand and Feminism: An Unlikely Alliance."[14] Other commentators, such as James T. Baker and Ronald E. Merrill, have recognized the potentially feminist qualities of Rand's female lead characters, but because Rand describes femininity in terms of "hero worship" her status as a feminist is denied.[15] Recently, however, a compendium of essays—*Feminist Interpretations of Ayn Rand*—has emerged that discusses all aspects of Rand's feminism (or lack thereof).[16] As one might imagine, the "rape" scene from *The Fountainhead* gets some attention. Prior to *Feminist Interpretations of Ayn Rand,* some commentators, like Susan Brownmiller and Ulrike Heider,[17] found the scene indicative of an antifeminist slant in Rand because it places women in such a subservient, masochistic role. Newer commentators such as Wendy McElroy see the scene as consensual and thus as allowing women a self-defining sexuality that is not reducible to either traditional or "rape culture" conceptions of sexuality.

The "rape" scene, however, is hardly the whole of the controversy surrounding Rand on the issue of feminism. There are broader issues as well. Brownmiller again, along with Lynda Glennon and others, regard Rand's writing and philosophy as being male *in general.* Rand's reason-centered philosophy, coupled with her advocacy of self-interest, emotional control, and instrumentalist rationalism, give her ideas and style a curiously "male" quality that is opposed to the organic, holistic, and dialectical modes favored by feminist writers and thinkers. Whether Rand is adequately characterized by the foregoing nonfeminist categories is open to some question. John W. Robbins has claimed that Rand employs dialectical thinking, and Chris Sciabarra has argued at length that Rand is a superior dialectician and synthetic thinker.[18] Others, such as Barry Vacker and Valerie Loiret-Prunet, see some of the "objectionable" qualities of Rand's writing and thinking as surface characteristics that mask other qualities that would be more appealing to feminists if they were not themselves blocked by ideological blinders.

The ideological blinders are nevertheless significant in explaining why feminists have given Rand so little attention. Those sympathetic to Rand—such as Nathaniel Branden, Wendy McElroy, and Joan Kennedy Taylor—wish to carve out an individualist feminism that is consistent with some form of the classical liberal politics Rand advocates. Can there be, in other words, a feminism that is not tied to left-leaning political doctrines? In this respect, the topic of feminism feeds naturally into our second topic of individualism.

One approach to resolving the tension between individualism and feminism is to deny that there can be a connection between them. For some, such as David Kelley and Ronald Merrill,[19] feminism is an inherently collectivist concept, since it perceives people in terms of group membership rather than individual characteristics. This perspective is contrary to Rand's philosophy and should be discarded. Others would agree that the two concepts of individualism and feminism are opposed but would advocate the rejection of individualism. Some commentators, such as Estelle Jelinek,[20] argue that individualism in Rand—as evidenced by *The Fountainhead*'s contrast between the heroes and the masses—reduces to an elitism unacceptable to radical feminists. But this perspective on the characters represents one extreme not necessarily shared by other commentators (e.g., Sharon Presley, Susan Love Brown, and Diana Brickell) featured in *Feminist Interpretations of Ayn Rand*. These commentators see some value for feminism in the independence and competence the leading female characters exhibit, even if they find other things to criticize in Rand's portrayal of women.

Rand's individualism, then, lends ambiguity to her feminism, depending on one's view of the nature of feminism. Ambiguity does not rest only with her view of women, however. Her commitment to or understanding of individualism has been criticized as well. The "official" view is that individualism is necessitated by the fact that thought or reason—which stands at the center of Rand's philosophy—is an attribute of individuals and individuals alone.[21] One of the earliest and most well known of the criticisms that Rand was consistently individualistic was given by Albert Ellis, who argued that Rand's philosophy may claim to be individualistic but produces instead a kind of religious-cult mentality among its followers.[22] The argument is not simply that her followers are devoted to her, but rather that the nature of the doctrine itself demands conformism. A humorous satirical expression of a similar criticism is contained in Jerome Tuccille's *It Usually Begins with Ayn Rand*.[23] More philosophically, some writers—beginning with Eric Mack[24]—have pointed to Platonic elements in Rand's thought. In other words, Rand's portrayal of characters as philosophical archetypes leads her away from actual individuals and toward individuals that exist only as ideas or ideally. This criticism is not unrelated to the previous one, for real individuals would get their individualism in this view by imitating the ideal forms of conduct exhibited by the characters Rand creates or by Rand herself. The end effect of this imitation is, of course, actually to deny individualism, if individualism means independent thought and action.

In academic literature, the issue of individualism is at least partially translated into a debate over the adequacy of Rand's ethics of "ethical egoism." Ethical egoism is the doctrine that our primary, and perhaps only, obligation is to ourselves, not to others. Individualism seems allied to ethical egoism because of its stress on personal independence. To be that independent may require that we think of ourselves first and foremost. The role others come to play in our lives is thus problematic, at least in the sense of how important they should be to us. Some commentators, such as O'Neill (1971), Baker (1987), and Robbins (1974), see Rand as lacking in benevolence or charity toward others or as fostering an elitist disdain for the well-being of others. Others, such as Erickson (1997), see altruism as a complicated notion Rand did not well delineate. Her defenders, by contrast, would argue that her ethic requires one neither to ignore others nor to act at their expense.

For those who have defended Rand directly on ethical topics (such as Mack, Machan, Peikoff, Rasmussen and Den Uyl, and Branden) or those who have written works inspired by her positions (such as Gotthelf and Lennox, Miller, Kelley, Hospers, Smith, and others[25]), individualism is rooted in principles of successful living. The terms *egosim* and *selfishness* apply in the sense that the individual's own values and goals are given a central place in the theory. This does not necessarily require that others be ignored or sacrificed to one's own interests. For example, the pledge members of "Galt's Gultch" take in *Atlas Shrugged,* that "I swear by my life and love of it that I shall never live for the sake of another man nor ask another man to live for mine," is a call to independence and voluntarism, not isolation and plunder. Others are not asked to live for their own sake because all associations are to be voluntary. To force another to do one's bidding would be to act as if that other were to live for his or her own sake. And one does not live for the sake of others in the sense that one must never abandon one's own independent judgment for the wishes, interests, or ends of others. One might, of course, judge it appropriate to join with others in pursuit of values one deems worthy. This idea of independent judgment and action is quite central to the individualism portrayed in *The Fountainhead*. The success of someone like Roark and the destructive consequences of people like Keating, Wynand, and Toohey are directly proportionate to their independence of thought and action.

Although some sympathetic commentators such as Erickson (1997) regard the notion of "life" as incomplete in Rand, all would seem to agree that for her individualism is a life-centered idea. Life is a phenomenon relegated to individuals, not to groups or collectivities. In her nonfiction works (e.g., *The Virtue of Selfishness*), Rand argues that life is the basis of all value, that is, in a fundamental sense things can make a difference only to that which faces the alternative of life or death. Rand's ethics are an effort to infer from these basic principles others that can guide one in successful living. Any inferred principles must nevertheless be true to their foundations, and that means that life and the values achieved in it are due to the actions and reflections of individuals. Rand's individualism is thus portrayed as being in the service of life, while alternatives are characterized as promoting the opposite. This does not make the doctrine any less controversial, but it may suggest that Rand's individualism is not so easily reduced to ordinary understandings of the term. Moreover, the doctrine is in principle open to arguments about the role others might play in successful living. In any case, we take up the issues associated with individualism and various aspects of Rand's ethics in other chapters to follow.

Rand's individualism, like most of the ideas associated with her, is rooted in an overall philosophy. That philosophy may not have been fully articulated when *The Fountainhead* was written, but the novel is nonetheless expressive of it. We need, therefore, to explore how Rand's philosophy figures into her art. The chapters that follow are an attempt to help that process along. Our perspective is to consider Rand's art and her philosophy as one and to understand—and criticize—each from the point of view of the other. Ayn Rand deserves to be ranked among the top 10 women of the twentieth century. It is quite possible that *The Fountainhead* should be counted among this century's great novels.

A READING

4

A Philosophical Novel

Ayn Rand has been described, and described herself, as a "novelist/ philosopher." This term is not as descriptive as it may seem, for virtually all great novelists employ philosophical themes and at least imply philosophical principles.[1] It is also quite likely that many authors are self-conscious about how their art incorporates philosophical issues and principles. A Jane Austen novel may seem at first to be simply about romance and marriage, but a deeper inspection reveals philosophical themes about human motivation, art and nature, reason, and emotion.[2] Of course, Rand never claimed she was the *only* novelist/ philosopher. Still, her fiction seems somehow distinctive. We need to first identify some of the novel's basic characteristics that make it a philosophical novel. Then we need to look at some of the features that give Rand's work its distinctiveness.

I

The Fountainhead is a novel about ideas. It appears to be a novel about architecture, but architecture is only the subject chosen to express the ideas. Given some of the ideas we shall be exploring throughout our discussion, architecture as a subject had certain advantages for Rand's purposes. Architecture blends nicely the artistic on the one hand and the scientific or technological on the other. Architecture is creative and requires an aesthetic vision, thus incorporating the artistic. But since one is dealing with a physical structure when one creates a building, engineering principles, at least, come into consideration. Rand's heroes are creative innovators whose precise understanding of reality makes it possible for them competently to shape their environment. Architecture simultaneously incorporates the creative, innovative, and knowledge-based aspects of human life.

Architecture also had another advantage for Rand. Its products are very public. They are out in the open for all to see. One of the themes of this novel is the individual versus the collective. The individual in question—Howard Roark—is made very visible by his creations, since they are displayed in public. All conflicts surrounding Roark's work themselves become very public. Roark's buildings, for example, get discussed in the city newspaper, the *Banner,* itself a vehicle for public opinion. Indeed, three of the novel's major characters are involved with the *Banner:* Dominique Francon, who writes a column on architecture; Ellsworth Toohey, who does likewise; and Gail Wynand, who owns the paper. Of the main characters besides Roark, only Peter Keating has no association with the *Banner.* The public nature of architecture and the representation of the public response to it by means of a newspaper give all the characters of this novel very noticeable roles in their community. That prominence makes any contrast between individual and community all the more dramatic.

It is worth noting in discussing this connection that when Rand was writing *The Fountainhead,* so-called modern architecture was still somewhat controversial. Some of Rand's characters may resemble actual architectural pioneers. Henry Cameron, Roark's mentor in the novel, may have been patterned after Louis Henry Sullivan (1856–1924), an American architect known for his influential dictum "Form follows function." The character of Roark was to some extent influenced by the American architect Frank Lloyd Wright (1869–1959).[3]

These real historical individuals undoubtedly faced many of the same social attitudes toward their work as Cameron and Roark do.

But it is equally important to understand that *The Fountainhead* is not a defense of modern architecture. Again, it is the ideas that matter to Rand, not architecture per se. A novelist wants to present information competently, and Rand spent a lot of time researching architecture. But it would not matter much at all if *The Fountainhead* were somehow defective in presenting the world of architecture as it really exists. That is not its point.

We know from the plot of the novel that Howard Roark is a brilliant young architect uninterested in re-creating the past. Rather, he wishes to build according to his own plans and specifications. The opinions of others, including that of most other architects, do not matter to him, nor do architectural commissions that allow others to alter his designs. He is also surprisingly uninterested in wealth, social status, or comfort. These attitudes give Roark an individualist posture that is the literary expression of the general idea of individualism. Roark's individualist attitude is also the fuel that drives the novel. As we shall see in the next chapter, each character embodies certain ideas or principles, but all are in one way or another responding to Roark. The basic response has to do with the theme of whether the individual must be subordinated to society or can stand apart, like Roark, even in defiance. Those who derive their worth from the opinions of others or who believe that worthiness is itself strictly social are opposed to Roark, even frightened by him. Those who think there might be some objective properties to worthiness and who believe that another's judgment should never be substituted for one's own are Roark's sympathizers. These classes of people conflict with one another in the novel in what constitutes the fundamental clash between good and evil. Individualism is the good, collectivism is the evil. The tension between the two fuels the action of the novel.

The theme of the individual versus the collective is most often represented, as are virtually all the novel's themes, by the characters of the novel. What happens in the novel is the result of the choices these individuals make. For reasons noted elsewhere in this chapter and in the next, character is critical to Rand's fiction. Character drives the action, not the reverse. But this novel seems *philosophical* because we grasp that the characters and their actions are representing ideas. These ideas are often perennial issues in philosophy. The individual versus the collective is a philosophical issue at least as old as the Athenian condemnation of Socrates. Furthermore, Rand has a particular take on this issue, one that we shall discuss in various ways as our interpretation proceeds. Consequently, to say that *The Fountainhead* is a philosophical work means both that it is a novel about ideas of a philosophical nature and that it offers a philosophy about those ideas.

Returning to the individual versus the collective, one should not make the mistake of seeing this contrast as one between those who think the individual should be subordinated to society and those who believe society should be subordinated to certain individuals. Critics of Rand sometimes wish to interpret her views this way, but this interpretation is quite mistaken. Rand considers the conflict between individual and collective to be between those who would subordinate the individual to society (the collectivists) and those who see individuals as independent actors with the right to exist for their own sake (the individualists). Interestingly, Rand places those who want to subordinate society to the individual in the group of nonindividualists or among the collectivists. She does so because these people want power over society, and seeking that sort of power reduces real individuals to mere segments of a collectivity to be mastered. Gail Wynand has something of this sort of collectivism in him.

The foregoing point raises another theme of the novel, the issue of power. The collectivists want power. We've mentioned Wynand, but the most power-oriented man in the book is Ellsworth Toohey. Toohey embodies the idea of subordinating the individual to the collective. Rand thinks of this subordination as a feature of "altruism"—a term of condemnation for her and one we shall explore later. Whatever the term, the collectivist lust for power is contrasted with the individualist's desire for independence and freedom. The contrasts, as we shall see, have all sorts of ramifications for the issue of the meaning and legitimate extent of power. In terms of the plot, Roark goes through much of the novel in an apparently powerless position. He has been virtually disenfranchised from his profession, and when he does get work it is either ignored or panned by critics. By the end of the novel, however, Roark is the most "powerful" man around, and his power derives from an inner strength of character and soundness of mind.

The conflicts and hardships Roark must endure are not, however, due to individualism seen simply as fierce independence and inner strength. Rand connects individualism to other ideas besides independence and fortitude, for example ideas about excellence and integrity. Keating goes to Roark for help because Roark is the most competent architect he knows. Roark is also the character most "together," most sure of himself and what he wants to do.

Roark struggles to get commissions on the basis of others recognizing his competence and vision as an architect and for no other reason. People who want him to compromise that vision confront him throughout the novel. They do not propose a better, alternative vision but rather seek to break down Roark's independent one. In other words, they wish Roark to compromise his integrity. The climax of the novel comes when Roark dynamites Cortlandt homes. Keating had originally gone to Roark because he was the only one competent enough to solve the architectural problem involved. But Roark's vision, both aesthetically and otherwise, was compromised by others who took over the project and altered his design. Bombing Cortlandt was a gesture that dramatically illustrated not only that fundamental compromise cannot be tolerated but also that integrity, excellence, and independence are all somehow connected to one another. We shall try to sort out some of that connection later on.

At this stage we can pause to note that the idea of personal integrity is a key concept in interpreting this novel correctly. Personal integrity is, I believe, the basis for explaining both independence and excellence, or is at least central to the meaning of each. One does not have personal integrity, for example, because one is skilled or competent; rather, the pursuit of excellence, of which skill and competence are a part, is a feature of one's personal integrity. By the same token, real independence comes not from mere nonconformity but from being true to oneself—from personal integrity. Self-knowledge and action according to principle have a long history of being associated with personal integrity. Consequently, character development, as we shall see momentarily, is the means by which Rand's philosophy and her literary art are simultaneously expressed. It may seem strange at first, but to say that this is a novel about ideas is, for Rand, to say it is focused on people's characters.

There is, as a consequence of the centrality of character, what might be called a normative quality to this novel. Rand desires to present us with a moral ideal in the person of Howard Roark. He represents qualities Rand believes we should admire and aspire to ourselves. In that sense Roark is a kind of norm for us to follow. But unlike so many "feel good" novels and films of our era that also seek to inspire, the ideas associated with this particular moral ideal are controversial. Rand wrote a book entitled *The Virtue of Selfishness*. In that book she defends a theory of selfishness—a theory that Roark is supposed to embody. The term *selfishness* itself is controversial, and it is instructive for our purposes here to look at what she says about her use of the term in her introduction to that book:

> The title of this book may evoke the kind of question that I hear once in a while: "Why do you use the word 'selfishness' to denote virtuous qualities of character, when that word antagonizes so many people to whom it does not mean the things you mean?"
>
> To those who ask it, my answer is: "For the reason that makes you afraid of it."
>
> But there are others, who would not ask that question, sensing the moral cowardice it implies, yet who are unable to formulate my actual reason or to identify the profound moral issue involved.[4]

Much of our interest in someone like Roark is expressed by the questions this passage raises. Is Roark really selfish? If so, how can this be a good thing? If not, why does Rand insist on the term? If the idea of selfishness makes us uncomfortable, is the defect in Rand, or in us, or in our failure to understand the idea or Roark himself? The point here is not to answer these questions so much as to suggest that they are carried along with the ideal Rand presents to us in the person of

Roark. In chapter 7 we explore the ways in which Rand uses her art to give us fresh perspectives on certain ideas. For the purposes of this chapter, if philosophy pushes one to think in new and potentially controversial ways, then Roark's embodiment of this particular idea surely makes this a philosophical novel!

The Fountainhead, then, is a novel about ideas. It is about ideas in the sense of exhibiting them through characterization, plot, and action. It is about ideas in the sense that Rand advocates certain doctrines. It is also about them in the sense that they are explicitly discussed as ideas. Roark, Wynand, and Toohey all give generalized and abstract accounts of their motivations and values as ideas. We do not have to guess at their principles very often, for they are openly (at least to the reader) expounded and debated. These characters often behave like philosophers in that they seek to articulate positions in general terms on whatever they are addressing. Roark's speech during his trial at the end of the novel is an example, but there are plenty of other moments when the characters begin philosophizing. The reasons that the characters philosophize should become clear in a moment, but it is important to see that the themes we have discussed make philosophizing an integral part of the very structure of this novel.

II

Despite the remarks about philosophizing to this point, Rand was careful to put the term *novelist* before *philosopher,* even in light of her extensive nonfiction writings. Her emphasis was always on her art, and she spent the bulk of her efforts on producing and perfecting it. However tempting it might be to see the novel as the medium through which Rand expresses philosophical ideas, we must resist this temptation. The novel becomes simply an instrument of philosophy on this view, and that seems contrary to Rand's own conception of what she is doing.[5] It is more plausible to say that the philosophical principles in which Rand is most interested can take their final shape, and thus their final meaning, only within the fictional, or at least literary, form. The reasons this should be so are obscure at first, because philosophical principles would seem to be just the sort of principles that have no necessary connection to the literary form. But Rand has a certain view of both philosophy and literature that renders the two particularly compatible. Her view of the appropriate nature of philosophy is what I shall call "socratic."[6] Her view of the appropriate form of art and literature is what she herself calls "romantic."

The line (from Plato's *Apology*) most famously associated with Socrates is that "the unexamined life is not for man worth living." Elsewhere in the same dialogue Socrates states that he goes about "persuading you, young and old, to care ... for ... [nothing] ... so much as excellence of soul."[7] Such statements, as well as Socrates' whole project of questioning, suggest that philosophy is first of all an intellectual activity in the service of human life—that is, of living well. Philosophy is neither an intellectual game nor a window to another reality but a discipline that reveals principles for human living. Philosophy is, because of this contribution to human life, essentially a *moral* enterprise and not, as it is usually interpreted, an analytical one—that is, it is not an enterprise in which ideas are analyzed to discover their logical connections to other ideas. It is more like a way of life than simply a theoretical exercise or discipline.

That Rand's view of philosophy is socratic in the foregoing sense is clear from a number of sources. In one of her letters, for example, the point about philosophy and human living is put simply: "[O]ur actions must be governed by abstract philosophical principles whenever we act as human beings and expect to achieve any rational goal."[8] Indeed, her nonfiction work *Philosophy: Who Needs It* is devoted entirely to arguing that philosophy is central to living well.

As to the moral character of the enterprise, Rand tells us in the introduction to the 25th-anniversary edition of *The Fountainhead* that her "purpose is *not* the philosophical enlightenment of [her] readers." Rather,

> the motive and purpose of my writing [is] the projection of an ideal man. The portrayal of a *moral ideal,* as my ultimate literary goal, as an end in itself—to which any didactic, intellectual or philosophical values contained in the novel are only the means. (ix; emphasis in original)

The key concept in this passage is "moral ideal." In these two words we are given a sense of Rand's unique way of integrating the philosophical and the aesthetic. The presentation of an "ideal" would seem to be simply a statement that the purpose of the work is aesthetic. But our point here is that the aesthetic cannot be separated or understood apart from the philosophical, interpreted in the socratic way just described—that is, as essentially moral. The moral in turn, as we shall see shortly, is itself caught up in a kind of aesthetic problem. The character of the aesthetic is thereby altered in Rand. Instead of the ideal being an object of disinterested contemplation, admiration, or emotional responsiveness normally associated with what it means for something to be "aesthetic," it is instead an object of personal transformation. That is to say, the ideal cannot remain outside of the reader as something to gaze upon. It becomes ideal only when the individual incorporates it as part of his or her own inner truth and motivation. This too is very socratic, for Socrates has us seek the ideal meaning of things, because doing so is critical to successful development of our character and consequently to success in human living.

The foregoing passage also leads us nicely into the second central feature of socratic philosophy: its perfectionism. Perfectionism here means not just an admonishment to "do better" but the idea that the standard for measuring the appropriate function of something comes from considering it in its perfected state. We might, for example, ask what it means to live a "human life." We could answer this question by considering an average of how most people actually live. Here we would arrive at something like "normal" life, and what was "normal" would function as a standard of evaluation on how well someone was doing in living a human life. Yet we could also approach this same question by looking at the issue in its best light, in this case imagining people at their best under the best circumstances or doing their best in whatever circumstances they are in. This approach takes the "perfected state" as the standard. From this perspective what is normal could be considered defective, because it fails to meet the conditions exemplified in the perfected state.

Rand's writings are replete with contrasts between what people are often actually like and what it is possible for them to do or become. Rand has sometimes been criticized for creating "black and white" characters, but stark contrasts are in keeping with her art and message. Since part of her point is to give us a vision of the best, we see that vision more clearly when it is contrasted to the worst or the mediocre. The contrast between the actual and the desirable, for example, leads some of the key characters (e.g., Dominique and Wynand) in *The Fountainhead* to be moved not to let a corrupt world bring its corruption to things of greatness and beauty. Dominique says to Toohey, for example:

> "You know, Ellsworth, I think the man who designed this should have committed suicide. A man who can conceive a thing as beautiful as this should never allow it to be erected. He should not want it to exist. But he will let it be built, so that women will hang diapers on his terraces, so that men will spit on his stairways and draw dirty pictures on his walls. He's given it to them and he's made it part of them, part of everything. He shouldn't have offered it for men like you to look at." (249)

This description of one of Roark's buildings is almost symbolic of the novel's underlying tension, for a central issue is whether the mediocrity and baseness people often exhibit will in the end triumph over excellence. Although characters like Dominique and Wynand have given up on the idea that excellence might one day prevail, they still judge all things in light of the standard of perfection. Indeed, their depth of disappointment in the world as they find it is a function of their preoccupation with this standard.

In classical socratic philosophy the benefits of rational living according to the standard of perfection were displayed in one's character and described as "virtue." The virtuous person possesses qualities not often found in others—personal integrity, clarity of purpose, stability of character, and a significant degree of independence.[9] These are the very same qualities Rand wishes to exemplify in her characters. The following passage from *The Fountainhead* is highly descriptive of this point:

> "I often think that [Roark is] the only one of us who's achieved immortality. I don't mean in the sense of fame and I don't mean

that he won't die some day. I think he is what the conception really means. You know how people long to be eternal. But they die with every day that passes. When you meet them, they're not what you met last. In any given hour, they kill some part of themselves. They change, they deny, they contradict—and they call it growth. At the end there's nothing left, nothing unreversed or unbetrayed; as if there had never been any entity, only a succession of adjectives fading in and out on an unformed mass. How do they expect a permanence which they have never held for a single moment? But Howard—one can imagine him existing forever." (470)

This passage indicates that the "perfected" state is both rare and difficult, though worthy of our aspiration. Realization of that aspiration depends on an understanding of what one is—one's nature or the "entity" spoken of in the passage. Here we come to the final element of socratic philosophy—objectivity.

Today we tend to believe that the world is pretty much what we make of it. In this view our world is defined either by society or by our subjective experiences. There is no independent reality to which we must conform that exists outside of the human perspective. There is also no human nature that determines the principles on which we should act, for the very idea of a human nature is also the idea that there is a reality outside of us independent of our thoughts, feelings, and perspectives. Objectivity seems especially far removed from individuality, which to the contemporary mind is often linked to simple diversity or distinctiveness. To express our individuality we should, as the phrase puts it, "do our own thing," which usually means doing pretty much what we want—all lifestyles being equally valid provided they do not harm others.

Classical socratic philosophy also holds that one should "do one's own thing," except that to be oneself requires a rather strict adherence to a regimen of the pursuit of truth and conformity to objective principles that perfect our nature as human beings. The idea here is that success in human living does not allow one to do *whatever* one feels like doing, for feelings are precisely not the standard for, but at most a measure of, success. Indeed, doing one's own thing in the contemporary sense would *not* be a case of being oneself but rather of being a slave to whatever appetite happened to be dominant at the moment. To "be oneself" one must be the author of one's actions, which was thought to stem from the guidance of reason rather than feeling or appetite.

Rand's individualism is in this socratic vein as well. In *The Fountainhead*, at least, the individualism is less intellectualistic (though we *are* told that "integrity is the ability to stand by an idea"(321)) and more oriented toward the transformation of one's surroundings than its classical counterpart: "[M]ost people build as they live—as a matter of routine senseless accident. But a few understand that building is a great symbol. We live in our minds, and existence is the attempt to bring that life into physical reality"(541). The transformation of the world around us must be done in accordance with its laws, so the effort to bring "life into physical reality" is not at all arbitrary. Neither, as it turns out, is the process of attaining personal integrity.

Selflessness is the enemy for Rand not simply because it means living through others but more fundamentally because it represents a denial of an objective reality—in this case a denial of one's own self or nature. Understanding who or what one is goes hand in hand with understanding the world around us—truth applied first and primarily to one's own case is what personal integrity rests on. And it is reliance on one's independent judgment that builds both personal integrity and an understanding of the world. We can perhaps best see the importance of independent judgment by looking at its opposite. In the following passage Wynand speaks of Peter Keating:

> "He's paying the price and wondering for what sin and telling himself that he's been too selfish. In what act or thought of his has there ever been a self? What was his aim in life? Greatness— in other people's eyes. Fame, admiration, envy—all that which comes from others. Others dictated his convictions, which he did not hold, but he was satisfied that others believed he held them. Others were his motive power and his prime concern. He didn't want to be great, but to be thought great." (633)

And more generally,

"And isn't that the root of every despicable action? Not selfishness, but precisely the absence of a self. Look at them. The man who cheats and lies, but preserves a respectable front. He knows himself to be dishonest, but others think he's honest and he derives his self-respect from that, second hand.... When you suspend your faculty of independent judgment, you suspend consciousness. To stop consciousness is to stop life. Second-handers have no sense of reality. Their reality is not within them, but somewhere in that space which divides one human body from another. Not an entity, but a relation—anchored to nothing." (633, 634)

These passages indicate that in a very basic and general or metaphysical sense one is selfless when one holds that oneself, and the things in the world around one, have no nature or independent identity. As to coming to *know* something (what philosophers call "epistemology"), one is selfless when others' judgments are substituted for one's own. And *ethically* one is selfless when one attempts to derive moral worth from the favorable opinions of others rather than from objective personal accomplishment. Selflessness, then, is that form of living that rejects the central elements of a socratic philosophy—the use of reason to understand a reality one must engage to transform it into one's conception of how it and oneself ought to be.

This socratic view of philosophy is nicely suited to Rand's view of what literature ought to be doing. In her book *The Romantic Manifesto* we are told, for example, that

> With altruism as the criterion of value and virtue, it is impossible to create an image of man at his best—"as he might be and ought to be." The major flaw that runs through the history of Romantic literature is the failure to present a convincing hero, i.e., a convincing image of a virtuous man.... The highest function of Romanticism [is] the projection of moral values.[10]

Apart from the obvious connection to perfectionism, one need understand only that *altruism* is another term for *selflessness* to see how the foregoing connects to our last paragraph.

Romanticism for Rand is "true" art, because art itself is "a selective re-creation of reality according to an artist's metaphysical value-judgments"(*RM*, 81).[11] In essence, the artist for Rand can either move somewhere on the romantic continuum or embrace a contradiction and adopt what Rand calls "naturalism." Naturalism denies man's volition, and thus the assertion of naturalism contradicts the very act of being an artist, which by the foregoing definition is dependent on volitional acts. The idea that an artist could be a kind of impartial spectator using selective focus to identify themes or ideas without necessarily endorsing them seems completely foreign to Rand. Either she does not believe such detachment to be possible or she regards that sort of posture to be outside the realm of art.

The validity of Rand's philosophy of art is not, in any case, our concern here. It is romanticism's inherent identification with human potential and moral choice that links it so centrally to the socratic philosophy we have been discussing. Although it is romanticism that gives expression to Rand's philosophy, her view of romanticism—that is, romanticism as it itself ought to function—is a feature of her socratic philosophy. We can perhaps see this best if we look at the central points of her criticisms of past Romantic writers.

Great Romantic writers of the past (e.g., Hugo and Dostoevsky) may have had what Rand calls a correct "sense of life," but they lacked an articulated philosophy. Their sense of life led them to rebel in the name of individual freedom against the arbitrary and detailed rules of "classicism." In this way, Romantic authors were able to affirm the centrality of volitional choice and thus morality in human life.

> The distinguishing characteristic of this top rank (apart from their purely literary genius) is their full commitment to the premise of volition in *both of its fundamental areas:* in regard to consciousness and to existence, in regard to man's character and to his actions in the physical world.... They are *moralists* in the most profound sense of the word; their concern is not merely with values, but specifically with *moral* values and with the power of moral values in shaping human character. (*RM*, 91)

But without an articulated philosophy, these authors tended to identify freedom or individuality in terms of feelings rather than reason. In doing so, Rand believes, they were "surrendering the banner of reason to their enemies." The first failing, then, of the Romantic genre in literature according to Rand is its placement of emotion or feeling over reason. This not only abandons what we have described as a central tenet of socratic philosophy but explains what Rand thought she was contributing to this genre.

Because Rand gives so much emphasis to the ordering of one's choices, plot and characterization take on critical roles in what she regards as the appropriate way to create literature. A good plot, for example, supports the integral connection between reason, choice, and action. Some Romantic writers, she claims, lost sight of the relationship between action and moral principles and focused on action alone.[12] This may make for exciting reading at times, but it contributes to the degradation or erosion of reason because it suggests that actions can be successful independently of the faculty that comprehends and integrates principles (reason). Another way in which the elements of plot or characterization are compromised is when unusual events but ordinary characters dominate a work of fiction. Here the message is that our characters are beyond our control, so we need events to make the work interesting.

Development of character is, as we have seen, central to the socratic view. Keeping in mind that Rand holds that the artist is *always* projecting an ideal, it is easy to see why she would object to the lack of concern for characterization in literature. The other side of the last problem is equally objectionable. Here the character gets developed, but circumstances or events beyond the character's control give the plot either a secondary importance or an overwhelming sense of tragedy. In this connection, Rand mentions the writer Lord Byron as exemplifying this fault. We can see, then, that for Rand the ideal form of romanticism would leave both "consciousness" and "existence" open to volitional choice and development.

The appropriate form of romanticism also includes the appropriate "sense of life," which for Rand is a positive and happy one. This is to be expected, since a central element of the socratic philosophy is the idea that the pursuit of perfection is conducive to human well-being and not antithetical to it. There is fiction that does not portray life as positive and happy, and that Rand allows within the purview of Romanticism—horror stories and realistic detective novels. But this sort of fiction can distort or conflict with the sense of life romanticism ought to promote, because it exemplifies the principle that the universe surrounding one is hostile to one's endeavors.

It is quite tempting at this point to criticize Rand as being overly optimistic and idealistic. In portraying heroes only at their best and with the most optimistic sense of life, Rand's fiction may appear to parody its own call never to evade reality and to describe the possible as it really is. What the difference may be between the possible and the *realistically* possible is an interesting question, both in itself and applied to fiction. Can Rand be claiming to use reason when she ignores all probabilities and depicts and projects only absolutes? If, in other words, *possible* means something that occurs only once a millennium, does one encourage or discourage the values associated with such a remote possibility when one portrays it? When does the projection of a possibility cease to be realistic and become idealistic?

Whether the possibilities of character, achievement, and action in Rand's fiction are remote enough to qualify as idealism may be a criticism she deserves and is certainly a question worth raising. But the question must be raised with a full comprehension of how radically normative—for better or worse—Rand's fiction is. *All* aspects of the fiction—from the setting and facial expressions to basic choices—serve the projection of values or principles. There is, therefore, almost nothing that is purely descriptive or concrete. The most detailed account of a natural landscape serves the projection of some principle or value. In this respect the world of the Randian novel is quite unlike the "real world," where we do, at least initially, confront what is not of our own making. Rand's complaint, therefore, that others undermine romanticism by inserting elements of the nonvolitional into their fictional worlds brings us back full circle to her view of art, which is that the artist must function otherwise.

We might conclude this chapter, therefore, by noting that what we have seen in Rand is the melding, if not the equation, of art and philosophy. While art and philosophy have the same end of human well-being, it would nevertheless seem that the artist and philosopher approach that end from rather different vantage points. But to look at it that way is to miss the final point: it is the *characters* Rand creates who exemplify the blend of art and philosophy, not the components of the process she uses to create them. The distinct tools of art and philosophy in the hands of the creator and author become inseparably one in a character created. This is so because the characters represent the opportunity we all have to re-create ourselves according to a conception of what we should become. This re-creation explains why Rand is an individualist in her novels and her philosophy. It is only in the human individual that there is the need to do something with one's character and life. The individual is artistic because what one becomes requires creative shaping. The individual is philosophical because the success of creativity requires that one understand what to become. Rand's novels are but a literary expression of philosophy and art conjoined in human action.

5

Characters as Ideas

In keeping with her belief in individualism, Rand divided *The Fountainhead* into four sections, each named after one of the book's main characters (Keating, Toohey, Wynand, and Roark). It is worth noting that there is no section of the novel devoted to Dominique, and this is the reason for our separate discussion of her in the next chapter. Here our purpose is to say something about each of the characters to whom a section of the book is devoted. First, a few general comments.

It is interesting that the sections on Keating and Toohey begin with Roark, but the sections on Wynand and Roark begin with them. In a way this prefigures the tension and drama of the novel, for the contrast between Keating and Roark, and Toohey and Roark must first be established to develop the main idea of the novel and to move the plot along. Wynand, on the other hand, battles mainly himself. Though in the end he too must be contrasted to Roark, friendship marks most of their time together. Wynand could have been like Roark, but he made choices that led him elsewhere. Keating and Toohey were Roark's opposites from the beginning.

The logic of the order of the sections also deserves some comment. It is the Keatings of the world that make the Tooheys possible.

Without what Rand calls "second-handers" (those who derive their worth through the opinions of others) like Keating, the collectivist philosophy and orientation of Toohey could not succeed. A good portion of Toohey's evil is his clear understanding of the connection between "second-handedness" and collectivism and his use of it for his own power. Toohey too is a second-hander, but of a vastly more complex and superior order than Keating. We see more clearly how one relates to the other by witnessing Keating first. That is, we see not only how easy it is to manipulate someone like Keating who has no internal source of self-worth but also how the power Toohey possesses is virtually handed over to him. Unlike Wynand, who tries to gain power by giving people what they want, Toohey more effectively gains it by wanting whatever they are willing to give. In Keating's case, Toohey collects Keating's entire sense of self-worth. So although Toohey ends up determining the contents of Keating's soul, chronologically it makes more sense to begin with Keating and then see how that condition of dependency develops.

Ignoring for the moment the story line, it is conceivable that the section on Wynand could have preceded the one on Toohey. After all, Toohey's form of power is an advancement over Wynand's, and Wynand in some respects eventually falls under Toohey's grasp. As a literary device, however, the failure of what appears to be the better strategy toward power—namely, Wynand's—is more effectively set off if it comes after we understand something fundamental about Toohey's form of power. The conventional forms of power—wealth, ownership, position, and influence—all give the reader the sense that Wynand is in command of the tools of power.

> "Okay," said Wynand, flicking the switch off. As his hand moved back, he noticed the row of buttons at the edge of his desk, bright little knobs with a color code of their own, each representing the end of a wire stretched to some part of the building, each wire controlling some man, each man controlling many men under his orders, each group of men contributing to the final shape of words on paper to go into millions of homes, into millions of human brains—these little knobs of colored plastic, there under his fingers. (540)

Rand even makes Toohey Wynand's employee to help continue the illusion that Wynand has superior control. In the end, of course, Wynand is no match for his own employee, and Toohey shows how ideas can more securely bind others than the materialistic weapons Wynand has at his disposal. All this would be much harder to see if we understood Wynand before Toohey.

It is rather obvious why Roark's section would have to be the last in a Romantic novel in which the good is to prevail. If Roark represents what is possible to human beings and the story displays the struggle and triumph of that possibility, then the only suitable place is at the end of the novel. What is perhaps not quite as obvious is that the most significant philosophical speeches take place in the Roark section as well. In *For the New Intellectual,* a collection of important philosophical passages from Rand's novels, all the selections from *The Fountainhead* are from the Roark section of the novel. It is as if what seem to be little ideas and actions early on in the novel grow into big ideas and actions by the end.

Finally, it is worth noting that the section on Roark is the only section whose namesake does not appear as a child in his own section. We see Keating, Toohey, and Wynand in their youth, but not Roark. He is presented as a contemporary adult only. The bits concerning his childhood we do learn come in the other sections of the novel. One can only speculate about why this is so. Perhaps it is because Rand regarded historical development to be irrelevant to understanding an ideal. Perhaps she believed presenting Roark in his formative stages would lessen the purity of the ideal. No clear reason seems to present itself on this matter. In general, however, childhood in all the characters interests Rand only to the extent that it helps explain the adults. A further discussion of Roark as a child, therefore, might very well add nothing to our understanding by this point in the novel.

PETER KEATING

Peter Keating opens this novel because in many respects he is not too far from most of us. His corruption is our possible corruption, for it comes incrementally in little steps. Keating's corruption eventually ends in complete degradation. We have already noted that Rand sees Keating as a "second-hander." The two passages presented in the last chapter during our discussion of selflessness were passages about Peter Keating and the meaning of being a second-hander. While "second-hander" is the common term Rand and others use in reference to Keating, he could also be described as someone who cuts corners. Cutting corners and second-handedness reinforce one another—indeed, the former is the road to the latter. The little compromises of our integrity we make along the way—either to please others directly or to do what we can do better just to "get by"—are the steps by which the voids left in our integrity get filled by the opinions or approval of others.

Toohey understands the logic of the process of losing integrity and its ultimate price quite well. He describes it to Keating:

> "Make man feel small. Make him feel guilty. Kill his aspiration and his integrity. That's difficult. The worst among you gropes for an ideal in his own twisted way. Kill integrity by internal corruption.... Tell man that he must live for others. Tell men that altruism is the ideal. Not a single one of them has ever achieved it and not a single one ever will. His every living instinct screams against it.... Since the supreme ideal is beyond his grasp, he gives up eventually all ideals, all aspirations, all sense of his personal value. He feels himself obliged to preach what he can't practice. But one can't be good halfway or honest approximately. To preserve one's integrity is a hard battle. Why preserve that which one knows to be corrupt already? His soul gives up its self-respect. You've got him. He'll obey." (665)

Although the foregoing states the ultimate outcome, the passage suggests it is within our nature to struggle against that outcome. Unless we are as evil as Toohey, we lose the fight by degrees. Consequently, we are only dimly aware of second-handedness in Keating as the book begins. The propensity for being a second-hander is there. For example, while listening to graduation speeches Keating "knew that he was the hope and his was the future, and it was pleasant to hear this confirmation from so many eminent lips"(18). But this in itself is not corruption. One could be pleased to hear such things because of one's belief in one's potential. For Keating, however, hearing the praise is what matters, not doing what it takes to be worthy of praise. In this respect, Keating confuses the benefit of an action with its end (or replaces the latter with the former). The pleasure that comes from praise becomes the end, and Keating cuts corners to achieve it.

We see Keating cutting corners for approval early on. He allows his mother to push him away from art and toward architecture. Later he wins the prize to attend the Paris Academy of Beaux-Arts but chooses to work for Guy Francon instead. Though this choice was the lesser of two evils from Roark's perspective, it nevertheless represents a further compromise of integrity on Keating's part. For him the more compelling yet more difficult and riskier task would have been to pursue art, but working for Francon offered immediate prestige. Later in the novel, Keating takes up painting again, but it is too late to recapture what could have been had he only been true to himself. We know from Roark that Keating had some talent (24), but that talent made it easier for him to "get by" rather than urging him toward excellence.

Rand's style of writing in absolute terms can give the impression that someone like Keating is from the outset a thorough mediocrity in every capacity. His talent lies only in his social skills and nowhere else. Though this interpretation is plausible and often fits with the text of the novel, it should be resisted. Apart from any realism that may be gained by supposing that Keating could not have gotten so far even in a corrupt world without some real talent, resisting the temptation to read Keating as an absolute mediocrity actually drives home Rand's point better. For if whole persons are either completely mediocre or completely brilliant, then their choices have to be similarly mediocre or brilliant, making the chance for self-improvement in any meaningful sense unlikely. But if we see Keating as compromising what could have been developed in alternative directions, we see more clearly that this is the sort of choice that we all face at every turn.

Keating's incremental corruption is most clearly demonstrated in two areas: his relationship with Catherine, and the early stages of his career. It is clear that he felt something real for Catherine: "Katie . . . I'll never love anyone else" (49). Indeed, "he wanted her; she loved him and had admitted it simply, openly, without fear or shyness, asking nothing of him, expecting nothing; somehow, he had never taken advantage of it"(45). Moreover, "he felt at peace. He felt he had nothing to fear, in this house or anywhere outside" when he was with her (46). Rand is undoubtedly suggesting that Keating loves Catherine because she, like him, is not possessed of great self-esteem and is prone to the corrupting influences of her uncle Ellsworth Toohey. She is certainly safe and nonthreatening, and her admiration for Peter Keating is genuine. In this respect, then, Keating pursues not a great love but a comfortable one. Nevertheless, the feeling between them is genuine and represents something both compromise away.

Keating's compromise is more despicable, but retrievable; Catherine's is more innocent, but hopeless. The critical moment for Keating comes when he has promised to return the next day and marry Catherine but instead goes ahead and marries Dominique, whom he does not love but who will give him more prestige and status. Catherine is simply jilted without explanation, but later Keating recognizes his error and comes to understand something important about the cumulative effect of incremental compromises:

> "Katie, I wanted to marry you. It was the only thing I ever really wanted. And that's the sin that can't be forgiven—that I hadn't done what I wanted.... Katie, why do they always teach us that it's easy and evil to do what we want and that we need discipline to restrain ourselves? It's the hardest thing in the world—to do what we want. And it takes the greatest kind of courage. I mean what we really want. As I wanted to marry you. Not as I want to sleep with some woman or get drunk or get my name in the papers. Those things—they're not even desires—they're things people do to escape from desires—because it's such a big responsibility, really to want something." (626)

Catherine, by contrast, has betrayed herself to the point where her innocence has become completely corrupt. She, of course, could not be responsible for Keating's conduct, but her innocent, simple nature is transformed by the altruistic philosophy of her Uncle Ellsworth. By the time of the scene from which the previous passage was taken, Catherine has lost her soul.

"I loved you, Katie."

She looked at him—and she seemed pleased. Not stirred, not happy, not pitying; but pleased in a casual way. He thought: If she were completely the spinster, the frustrated social worker, as people think of these women, the kind who would scorn sex in the haughty conceit of her own virtue, that would still be recognition, if only in hostility. But this—this amused tolerance seemed to admit that romance was only human, one had to take it, like everybody else, it was a popular weakness of no great consequence—she was gratified as she would have been gratified by the same words from any other man—it was like that red-enamel Mexican on her lapel, a contemptuous concession to people's demand of vanity. (626)

Whatever genuine simple humanity Catherine possessed is gone. She has become a kind of artificial creation of her own circumstances and Toohey's philosophy. Normal human desires were a sign of selfishness. Catherine has now become selfless, not simply in her career choice to serve others rather than herself, but in the more immediate sense of escaping herself: "I'm so busy, I have to go so many places, ... but when they shoot me out to New York again, I'll ring you up, so long, Peter, it was ever so nice"(628).

Keating's other critical compromise comes early in his career. His interest is not in becoming a good architect but in climbing the ladder of success. He will do the work of others if it will help him get ahead, but what interests him is career and social climbing through corporate schmoozing and scheming.

But Heyer surprised everybody by remembering Keating's name and by greeting him, whenever they met, with a smile of positive recognition. Keating had had a long conversation with him, one dreary November afternoon, on the subject of old porcelain. It was Heyer's hobby; he owned a famous collection, passionately gathered. Keating displayed an earnest knowledge of the subject, though he had never heard of old porcelain till the night before, which he had spent at the public library. Heyer was delighted; nobody in the office cared about his hobby, few ever noticed his presence.

In the drafting room, Keating concentrated on Tim Davis. Work and drawings were only unavoidable details on the surface of his days; Tim Davis was the substance and shape of the first step in his career. Davis let him do most of his own work; only night work at first, then parts of his daily assignments as well; secretly at first, then openly. Davis had not wanted it to be known. Keating made it known. When Tim Davis lost his job, no one in the drafting room was surprised but Tim Davis. . . . He felt he had no friend on earth save Peter Keating. (57, 58)

Later, when work becomes "inconvenient" to his pursuit of success, Keating has others do his work for him. The final outcome is, of course, the disaster that finally occurs when Roark covers up for him one too many times with the Cortlandt homes.

Peter Keating is, in short, one model of how to compromise and lose one's integrity. From what we have said, we might label this "incremental second-handedness." It is a form of corruption no more excusable than any other but perhaps at times more understandable. Because it never reaches the depths of evil found in someone like Toohey, it is more pathetic. Keating is someone we almost feel sorry for in the end, not so much because we excuse his choices but because he is an example of a life wasted. As Dominique puts it, "Some day you'll know the truth about yourself too, Peter, and it will be worse for you than for most of us"(255).

ELLSWORTH TOOHEY

Ellsworth Toohey, by contrast, does not seem to have arrived at his condition incrementally. Like Roark, he is someone who is not defeated in the end. Though Roark triumphs, Toohey neither disappears nor alters his patterns of life in any way. He is always in the background, because triumphs like Roark's need to be repeated constantly. However much Peter Keating may recede in potency, Toohey is always there to be dealt with. Indeed, it is Rand's point that Toohey's power grows as Keating's recedes. It is a power that is derived, not intrinsic. Toohey gets his power from what people like Keating give him, not from an inner source of strength or virtue. Consequently,

Toohey is always there because the little compromises others are willing to make—the stuff of Toohey's own power—are always there.

Toohey is a second-hander for more pernicious reasons than Keating. Whereas Keating wants fame and attention, Toohey wants to collect human souls and use their power to destroy what is good. One cannot help but wonder if the name Ellsworth is a pun on "else worth." Toohey offers others who must find their worth elsewhere a sense of what they seek. By the same token, he gathers his own strength from the worth others have moved elsewhere—that is, from themselves to him. To destroy what is worthwhile and capture that power for oneself requires that other individuals alienate their own worth.

> "What do you ... want ... Ellsworth?"
> "Power, Petey."
> "I shall rule."
> "Whom ... ?"
> "You. The world. It's only a matter of discovering the level. If you learn how to rule one single man's soul, you can get the rest of mankind. It's the soul, Peter, the soul. Not whips or swords or fire or guns. That's why the Caesars, the Attilas, the Napoleons were fools and did not last. We will. The soul, Peter, is that which can't be ruled. It must be broken. Drive a wedge in, get your fingers on it—and the man is yours. You won't need a whip—he'll bring it to you and ask to be whipped. Set him in reverse—and his own mechanism will do your work for you. Use him against himself." (664, 665)

In handing over one's self-worth—either because one's soul has been broken or because one has accepted an altruistic philosophy—one gives to people like Toohey the whip as one asks for the whipping.

Toohey is not, however, passive when it comes to strengthening his power. He does not wait to be handed the souls of others. He actively seeks to break their spirit. In the following telling passage he describes his method and how he might use it against Roark:

> "Now, I don't think that Roark thinks very much of Peter's work. He never has and he never will, no matter what happens. Follow this a step further. No man likes to be beaten. But to be beaten by the man who has always stood as the particular example of medioc-

rity in his eyes, to stand by the side of this mediocrity and to watch it shoot up, while he struggles and gets nothing but a boot in his face, to see the mediocrity snatch from him, one after another, the chances he'd give his life for, to see mediocrity worshiped [*sic*], to miss the place he wants and to see the mediocrity enshrined upon it … well, my little amateur, do you think the Spanish Inquisition ever thought of a torture to equal this?" (274–75)

This passage, among the others we have examined from Toohey, clearly indicates that Toohey knew what he was about. Attack on someone's self-esteem is the most powerful weapon of control. Toohey is a master at manipulating people and situations to undermine self-esteem. He has articulated to himself very clearly both his overall strategy and his tactics in particular cases.

Many of Rand's major characters, whether good or evil, are very self-conscious about their activities and goals. Little is hidden from the reader's view. Whereas some authors would prefer to keep their deeper themes less visible, Rand leaves little to interpretation when it comes to thematic presentation through major characters. This is perhaps another way of saying her novels are philosophical. It is certainly a way of expressing philosophical principles through characterization.

The self-conscious quality of Toohey's choices began at an early age. He learned how to use his physical frailties to manipulate people, how to play on their weaknesses to his advantage, and how to use "moral superiority" to cast doubt on the worth of others. This last point is illustrated by the following:

It happened that Pat Noonan offered Ellsworth a bag of jelly beans in exchange for a surreptitious peek at his test paper. Ellsworth took the jelly beans and allowed Pat to copy his test. A week later, Ellsworth marched up to the teacher, laid the jelly beans, untouched, upon the desk and confessed his crime, without naming the other culprit. All her efforts to extract the name could not budge him; Ellsworth remained silent; he explained only that the guilty boy was one of the best students, and he could not sacrifice the boy's record to the demands of his own conscience. He was the only one punished—kept after school for two hours. Then the teacher had to drop the matter and let the test marks remain as they were. But it threw suspicion on the grades of Johnny Stokes, Pat Noonan, and all the best pupils of the class, except Ellsworth Toohey. (304)

During his childhood Rand has Ellsworth attach himself to those doctrines useful in manipulating people—specifically religion and socialism. They are both useful because both advocate the alienation of self to some greater being or cause. Toohey knew the power self-alienation would give him, and thus he knew the power of these doctrines and how to use them.

Religion and socialism are for Rand altruistic doctrines, thus making Toohey Rand's symbol of the meaning of altruism. Rand does not regard altruism as an innocent doctrine of kindness and goodwill; it is a vicious doctrine designed to purge from people what is best within them. Rand has this view of altruism because she believes it to be the doctrine not just of placing others before self but of giving others moral *priority* over self. To alienate to another any part of an individual's potential for excellence, or to collectivize it, is to undermine the principle that is central to the production or promotion of what is good. The good comes only from one's own *individual* effort. Even actions that must be undertaken in consort with others are dependent on the efforts of individuals. Toohey either embodies or feeds off of all such perversions of self. In this respect, Toohey is perhaps Rand's most evil character. In *Atlas Shrugged* altruism is more diffused across society. In this novel it is as if one person embodies it all.

There is the suggestion in Rand's depiction of Toohey that those who seek power over others invented altruism, since evil has no power of its own and must contrive a way to get others to give theirs up. In addition, one of Rand's points in this book is that evil is impotent in the face of good. The idea here is that Toohey's power comes from what others give to him and that he has no intrinsic power of his own. But we also noted that Toohey was not passive in the development of his power. Are these conceptions of Toohey consistent? It would seem that Toohey's self-conscious pursuit of power could hardly be thought of as impotence. By the same token, it would be problematic for Rand to give positive power to evil, because that would undermine Rand's metaphysical optimism—a theme we discuss in chapter 8. We can say here, however, that the problem with giving Toohey (and those like him) positive power in his own right is that Dominique's final realization—that all she needed to do was do what Roark did and stand up to evil—would be less certain of success. Giving Toohey power would also have the effect of making Dominique's project with respect to Roark morally problematic. Some difficulties with Dominique's project are discussed in the next chapter, but we can see here that the moral issue becomes particularly acute if evil could defeat Roark in some *fundamental* way. In other words, if evil could finally triumph over good, then it is hard to justify ever abandoning the defense of the good for any reason and for any amount of time, let alone trying to undermine it as Dominique does with Roark. Finally, another problem with giving evil positive power is that it would diminish the centrality of character and choice. Noble characters and intelligent choices might not be enough for success in the face of an inherently powerful evil.

We might be inclined to solve our problem by claiming that the evil characters of Rand's later novel *Atlas Shrugged* are more consistent. They are uniformly more cowardly and less calculating than Toohey and therefore fit better with the thesis about the inherent impotence of evil. Toohey, however, captures our imagination better (is any character of Rand's more memorable?) and certainly rings at least as true to life, if not truer, than the villains of *Atlas Shrugged*. Consequently, it would seem most appropriate to leave the problem open and label it simply "Rand's problem of evil." Toohey is enigmatic because evil is enigmatic, and no one is more evil than Toohey.

GAIL WYNAND

Gail Wynand at first seems different from Toohey altogether. If Toohey is the altruist, Wynand, in common parlance, is the egotist. He seems to have no consideration for others and uses them as he pleases, whereas Toohey is *all* consideration. We have already noted Wynand's love of power. In addition—and here we do have a similarity to Toohey—he delights in breaking the will of others:

> Wynand lost interest in breaking industrialists and financiers. He found a new kind of victim. People could not tell whether it was a sport, a mania, or a systematic pursuit.... It began with the case of Dwight Carson. Dwight Carson was a talented young writer who had achieved the spotless reputation of a man passionately devoted to his convictions.... Wynand bought Dwight Carson. He forced Carson to write a column on the *Banner,* dedicated to preaching the superiority of the masses over the man of genius.... A few months later Wynand bought a young writer from a radical magazine, a man known for his honesty, and put him to work on a series of articles glorifying exceptional men and damning the masses. (429)

It is, however, too simplistic to say that Wynand was an egotist in love with power and wealth. Wynand concluded at an early age that there was no integrity in the world, and his endeavors to break the wills of people like Dwight Carson are as much for the sake of further confirmation of that thesis as they are delights in power. This must be so or the relative fit between Wynand and Dominique would not have seemed so convincing, since their motivations throughout the novel are not dissimilar. Moreover, Wynand's art collection and his friendship with Roark are other indications that he is not simply a boorish egotist but a man of some substance.

Wynand would also not fall outside of the purview of an altruist, although the usage here of the term *altruist* seems a bit strange. We already know that Wynand was motivated by the desire to control others, as Toohey was. Moreover, he gives people what they want (again, as does Toohey). Of course, what he delivers to them are their own vices:

> "Men differ in their virtues, if any," said Gail Wynand, explaining his policy, "but they are alike in their vices." He added, looking straight into the questioner's eyes: "I am serving that which exists on this earth in greatest quantity. I am representing the majority—surely an act of virtue?" (423)

The difference between Wynand and Toohey on this matter, then, is that whereas Wynand supports people's vices, people's vices support Toohey. This is the reason Toohey has more power than Wynand in the end; Wynand is finally a slave to those he believes he controls, because he caters to them. Toohey gets others to cater to him.

Wynand is not, consequently, altruism incarnate, as Toohey is. Though there are similarities and logical connections, it is still power, not altruism, that Wynand signifies. More precisely, it is the effect *on oneself* of power that Wynand comes to represent. We should recall that the section on Wynand opens with him contemplating suicide. It is the deadening of the soul that power produces: "One does not die like this, he thought. One must feel a great joy or a healthy terror. One must salute one's own end. Let me feel a spasm of dread and I'll pull the trigger. He felt nothing" (405). Though Roark and Dominique may enliven his soul as the novel progresses, in the end we see his soul deadened by its lust for power. He is unable to give up the only thing he has really built, namely the *Banner,* but what he has built requires that he give up himself.

We must read Wynand as a complicated figure with some good in him or it is difficult to reconcile Roark's friendship with him and Roark's opinion that "the worst second-hander of all [is] the man who goes after power"(636). Roark's friendship for Wynand is not a transitory one that ends in some discovery of what Wynand is really like. Roark remains true to Wynand until the end:

> "'Howard, you spoke about a house as a statement of my life. Do you think my life deserves a statement like this?'
> "Yes."
> "Is this your honest judgment?"
> "My honest judgment, Gail. My most sincere one. My final one. No matter what might happen between us in the future." (558)

Roark could not both retain respect for Wynand "no matter what might happen" and think one who pursues power the worst type of second-hander unless there was some sort of mitigating circumstance. In Wynand's case the circumstance is his failure to understand the way power corrupts excellence, for Wynand still loved excellence though he believed it either to be nonexistent or not long lived. Wynand cannot, therefore, be interpreted as more evil than Toohey. Rather, Roark's friendship simply adds to the tragedy of Wynand's fall.

HOWARD ROARK

Howard Roark would seem to be the easiest of the characters to sum up in terms of ideas. Rand's tendency as an author is to make her heroes increasingly more idea-like in proportion to the character's significance. The extreme of this is John Galt of *Atlas Shrugged,* described as a being of pure consciousness. We have already noticed that the important philosophical speeches in *The Fountainhead* are contained in the Roark section of the novel and that Roark comes to us in this section as fully adult. We learn little here, or elsewhere, about what shaped or motivated Roark—he seems always to have been the same. Things that may trouble others—expulsion from school, job insecurity, lack of recognition—seem to have little effect on Roark. In this Roark is most particularly the representation of self-sufficiency and integrity:

> "Gail, I think the only cardinal evil on earth is that of placing your prime concern within other men. I've always demanded a certain quality in the people I liked. I've always recognized it at once—and it's the only quality I respect in men. I chose my friends by that. Now I know what it is. A self-sufficient ego. Nothing else matters." (636)

Roark is undoubtedly also the embodiment of Rand's general moral and political ideals, namely egoism and capitalism, as well as the embodiment of particular virtues such as industry, creativity, honesty, productivity, and independence. Since Roark spends virtually all of his time working, he is easily represented by ideas—there is little else to him but the particularization of certain general theories or values.

But Roark is not thereby uninteresting as a person to the reader. Our interest in Roark is captured by more than an interest in the ideas he represents, for Roark's actions are not always the obvious implication of those ideas. Two mysterious facets of Rand's characterization of Roark draw us into him and the novel, the second of which we have already mentioned. The first mystery is Roark's willingness to do Keating's work despite his fierce belief in individualism. The second is his friendship with Wynand. We shall deal with the first of these issues in chapter 8. We need add to what we have already said about this last issue only that the triadic relationship between Roark, Wynand, and Dominique serves to give the reader a belief in the possible salvation of Dominique and Wynand while underscoring the idea of the corrupting nature of power. For the main difference between Dominique and Wynand is not in their love of Roark, which seems about equal, but the ways in which they have chosen to deal with the absence of excellence in the world. For Wynand it is the destruction of excellence in others. For Dominique it is that destruction in herself. In the end, however, others end up destroying Wynand, while Dominique's self is saved.

One important idea that we cannot ignore before closing is the idea of Roark as the embodiment of the correct theory of human progress. We find this view presented in Roark's courtroom speech:

> "Thousands of years ago, the first man discovered how to make fire. He was probably burned at the stake he had taught his brothers to light. He was considered an evildoer who had dealt with a demon mankind dreaded. But thereafter men had fire to keep them warm, to cook their food, to light their caves.... That man, the unsubmissive and first, stands in the opening chapter of every legend mankind has recorded about its beginning.... No creator was prompted by a desire to serve his brothers, for his brothers rejected the gift he offered and that gift destroyed the slothful routine of their lives. His truth was his only motive. His own truth, and his own work to achieve it in his own way.... He held his truth above all things and against all men. His vision, his strength, his courage came from his own spirit. A man's spirit, however, is his self." (710–11)

The individual makes advances for Rand—that is, individuals who live according to some inner truth or vision make advances. Mankind does not advance because of the work of society or any other collectivity. Ideas are what move the world, and while they can be shared, they originate and are advanced by individuals. Rand's argument, reminiscent of Plato's "Allegory of the Cave," is that ordinary society desires the familiar, and thus society is essentially conservative. People are comfortable with what they know, so innovation and advancement come from the one who breaks away from the crowd and lives by a new vision. Roark's work is strikingly original, and hence his treatment is a version of what is described in the passage above. But Roark wins his court battle and triumphs over all at the end of the novel. This is *not* in accord with what the foregoing passage describes. It raises the interesting question of what we should make of Roark's success when the historical treatment of innovators has been the one described in the foregoing passage. We shall take this question up again in chapter 8. It does not seem sufficient to respond to that question by simply saying that this is a romantic novel and as such requires a "happy ending." A more significant thesis is that Rand is also making a statement about good in the face of evil.

6

Dominique

Ayn Rand once described Dominique Francon as herself "in a bad mood."[1] Herein lies a source of the difficulty in interpreting what is really the central character of this novel. Rand herself might deny this last claim, arguing that Roark is the central character of the book because, as she says in one of her letters, Roark "exemplifies a man who has reached perfection."[2] But however perfect Roark may be, and however much he may represent the ideal that Rand wishes to portray, it is Dominique who traverses the four sections of this novel. As we have already noted, there is no separate section of this novel devoted to Dominique. Instead, she pervades them all. In many respects, Roark, Wynand, Toohey, and Keating are like satellites around her.

It is not that one must first understand Dominique to grasp what these men are; rather, it is through Dominique that the reader comes to understand these men and thus what finally can be said about Dominique. Though the novel is not written from Dominique's perspective, it is nonetheless through her eyes that the reader sees its world.[3] If Dominique is Rand in a bad mood, so then is the reader.

The standard—and not wholly incorrect—reading of Dominique is that she is a woman who withdraws from the world out of a sense of idealism or loyalty to excellence, which she will not allow to be sullied by the mediocrity of the world around her. She seeks, therefore, to destroy the man she loves before that world destroys him or (in what amounts to the same thing) before his greatness goes unappreciated, ignored, or defiled. Dominique's motivation, even if a bit extreme, is a common enough attitude stemming from a desire to preserve and protect something one loves. We would, for example, wish to prevent a person, thing, or idea we loved from being subjected to mocking or ridicule or mistreatment from an ignorant horde. And perhaps if we thought the situation extreme enough, we might wish to do *everything* in our power to prevent that possibility. In this respect, the device of pitting Dominique against Roark is a good one for setting up some dramatic tension in the novel. It is, nevertheless, a device that seems not fully consistent with some of Rand's own views.

The first problem is that Rand may see romance for a woman as surrender to a man.[4] Apart from wondering why a woman as self-sufficient and strong willed as Dominique would surrender to any man, and why romance cannot take place without either partner "surrendering" to the other, it is hard to imagine why one would devote an extraordinary amount of effort to destroying the life of the one to whom she is to surrender! The answer just given, that one wishes to protect what one loves, seems somewhat less than convincing with a character as strong and able as Roark to take care of himself and to assess his own risks. Roark does not need Dominique's protection, and one has to wonder why Dominique would not give him the benefit of the doubt and assume he knows all along what he is doing.

Of course, we could say that Dominique is trying to protect not Roark but rather herself, from having to witness what the world might do to Roark or, more plausibly, from having to witness its lack of appreciation of him. But it is hard to find much rationality in this. Wouldn't it make more sense to allow herself to appreciate and enjoy what Roark can accomplish, however limited and unappreciated it may be, than to destroy it before she can witness it? Does it really make sense to allow an idea (or its manifestation) to exist only when the environment for its reception is perfect and people will appreciate it as they ought? If Dominique were to succeed in destroying Roark, what exactly would she gain? Moreover, why would it not be worthier to fight for the cause, however hopeless, than to try to destroy it? Some of the discussion that follows will help address these questions, but it is clear that we need to examine other alternatives to the standard reading to make sense of Dominique.

One more plausible view of romance, one that also may be peculiar to Rand's own sense of romantic involvement, is the view in which the man "wins over" the woman by proving his worthiness. Instead of the inequality that surrender may imply, this interpretation, paradoxically, establishes the *equality* between Roark and Dominique. Dominique must test Roark to the maximum to ensure that he is good enough for her. To be that good, he must embody a perfection that finally can be established only by attempts to bring it down or destroy it. If Roark can pass these tests, he is indeed worthy of Dominique, for no test could be more stringent. She could then surrender to him. It is certainly hard to imagine Dominique settling for anything less than a man who could withstand the ultimate tests of character, so in this respect the reading fits. One sometimes finds hints of this romance-as-contest view in the text:

> "I [Dominique] have hurt you [Roark] today. I'll do it again. I'll come to you whenever I have beaten you—whenever I know that I have hurt you—and I'll let you own me. I want to be owned, not by a lover but *as an adversary* who will destroy my victory over him." (278; emphasis added)[5]

The only problem with this reading is that it flies a little too much in the face of the standard interpretation, since it is not idealism per se (not to mention "surrendering") that motivates Dominique. One cannot help but wonder whether Rand had some ambivalent attitudes toward the meaning of femininity as it applies to self-sufficient women.[6]

In a letter, Rand tells us that "the greatness of [Dominique's] love for Roark made her want to destroy him because she could not bear the thought of his existence in a world dominated by second-handers."[7] Rand also states in the same letter that Dominique "lost her fear of the world when she understood that it has never been and can never be dominated by the second-handers nor by the collective." This final realization must, of course, come at the end of the book; otherwise one could not understand Dominique's actions toward Roark if she knew ahead of time that genius must triumph. Nevertheless, there may still be some conflict in asking the reader simultaneously to believe that Dominique would want to keep Roark from second-handers and also that Roark must eventually triumph. We need to explore this a bit further.

First, Rand can be characterized only as an optimistic writer. This novel is about not just what is possible for human beings but also what is virtually inevitable, if human beings are to continue. Rand tells us, for example, that "the Tooheys will always go on—but they can never win."[8] This optimism is all the more remarkable in that historically it coincided with the collectivism of both Stalin and Hitler. Instead of reacting to the massive horrors of the twentieth century with despair, Rand provides a counsel of hope, and this may in part account for her continued popularity. But that counsel also makes it harder for us to comprehend Dominique. If such optimism is warranted, it is difficult to understand Dominique's extreme reactions. If the optimism is less certain, then it may not be correct to think of it as optimism. It is clear, however, that Rand is in fact optimistic. Why could not Dominique be so too?

It is one thing to say, as a philosophic abstraction, that human beings progress because of the efforts of those who are not second-handers and thus that the Tooheys will never win. It is quite another thing to say that the second-handers are not winning at the moment. As individuals we could be caught in the trough of the wave, however certain we are that the wave will eventually crest. This analogy would most assuredly describe the time in which this novel was written, and it can, I believe, help us understand the character of Dominique. The most plausible inference to draw from Rand's optimism and Dominique's extreme conduct is that Dominique is the only major character in this novel who learns anything and grows because of it! In this respect, our claim here is that she is much like the reader.

One commentator has described Dominique—for some of the reasons already given—as "the most unsatisfactory figure in the novel" and as a "symbol of idealism frozen by contempt."[9] But if our thesis is correct, Dominique is one of the least frozen characters of the book, for she learns and grows as the book progresses. Roark and Toohey are already "perfected" examples of their type. It might be argued that Keating and Wynand "progress" or learn or evolve, but in fact Keating *de*volves and Wynand only circles back to his starting point. Dominique is the only one who grows because of the insight she has gained.

It is also interesting to note that Dominique is virtually the only major character of the novel who does not give philosophical speeches but is capable of doing so. Peter Keating does not make philosophical speeches, but part of the point about his character is that he is neither prone to nor capable of such speeches. Obviously the same cannot be said of Dominique. She is certainly as capable as Wynand in this respect, and given Rand's own philosophizing, this sort of intellectual activity can hardly be the province of males only! It is especially odd that Dominique does not philosophize if she is an idealist, for one would expect that those ideals would be articulated at some point. Moreover, the other main characters get to articulate their visions and values.

It is not sufficient to argue in response that Dominique's ideals are articulated by Roark, because that would not explain why Dominique has given up on them while Roark has not. The more plausible conclusion, then, is that Dominique has not yet completely honed her principles or seen their full implication and interconnectedness. She has, in effect, a great deal to learn, as we witness from the following:

> "I wonder [Ellsworth] what you are—essentially. I don't know."
> "I dare say nobody does," he said pleasantly. "Although really, there's no mystery about it at all. It's very simple. All things are simple when you reduce them to fundamentals. You'd be surprised if you knew how few fundamentals there are. Only two perhaps. To explain all of us. It's the untangling, the reducing

that's difficult—that's why people don't like to bother. I don't
think they'd like the results, either."

"I don't mind. I know what I am. Go ahead and say it. I'm just
a bitch."

"Don't fool yourself, my dear. You're much worse than a
bitch. You're a saint. Which shows why saints are dangerous and
undesirable." (285)

The point is not that Dominique does not know what she wants
or that she is unclear about her values. She is a compelling mixture of
decisiveness and certainty on the one hand and the unconceptualized
on the other, as further evidenced in the following passage:

"Roark, I can accept anything, except what seems to be the easiest
for most people: the halfway, the almost, the just-about, the in-
between. They may have their justifications. I don't know. I don't
care to inquire. I know that it is the one thing not given me to
understand." (386)

Of course, if Dominique were to inquire into these things, she would
discover something of what she discovers in the end—namely, that
these compromises are a sign not of power but of weakness and that
second-handers do not provide the engine of progress. But Dominique
is perhaps where many of us are: we know that something is wrong
and that there are things we do not like, but it is not exactly clear to us
what may cause these things, or that we can make any difference, or
that the problem is not simply a necessary part of what is given to us.
She is like us also in that we may have a sense of what is right or worthy but are not so clear on how to articulate it or protect it, or why
others don't see it too.

It is perhaps no accident that Rand used the word *mood* in her
description of Dominique as herself. Dominique is the most intuitive
of the characters. She seems to operate more on insight and emotion
than on reason and analysis. We get this impression in part because
many passages about her are about her feelings toward Roark. Still,
one finds passages like the following:

She has always hated the streets of a city. She saw the faces streaming past her, the faces made alike by fear—fear as a common denominator, fear of themselves, fear of all and of one another, fear making them ready to pounce upon whatever was held sacred by any single one they met. She could not define the nature or the reason of that fear. But she always felt its presence. (247)

Although skewed a bit by Dominique's own project of destruction, the reader nonetheless gets much of the *emotional* power of the novel from the women—from either Rand herself as narrator or through the character of Dominique. Since Roark is the central hero of the book, Dominique's responses to him loom large as motivators for the reader within the story, just as the narrator's do from without. Dominique's emotional responses are directed primarily to Roark's architecture or to Roark himself. As for his architecture, we find passages like the following:

She thought, standing there in the heart of the building, that if she had nothing of him, nothing but his body, here it was, offered to her, the rest of him, to be seen and touched, open to all; the girders and the conduits and the sweeping reaches of space were his and could not have been anyone else's in the world; ... here was the shape he had made and the thing within him which had caused him to make it, the end and the cause together, the motive power eloquent in every line of steel, a man's self, hers for this moment, hers by grace of her seeing it and understanding. (293)

With respect to her love for Roark himself in light of her project of destruction, she says:

"Roark, there was a man talking to you out there today, and he was smiling at you, the fool, the terrible fool.... I wanted to tell that man: don't look at him, you'll have to hate the rest of the world, it's like that, you damn fool, one or the other, not together, not with the same eyes, don't look at him, don't like him, don't approve, that's what I wanted to tell him, not you and the rest of it, I can't bear to see that, I can't stand it, anything to take you away from it, from their world, from all of them, anything, Roark." (296)

From both these passages one begins to realize that the reader becomes Roark's lover through Dominique, and like Dominique we learn to *feel* Roark before we finally come to understand him fully.

Since there is no inherent philosophical contradiction for Rand between reason and emotion, Dominique's feelings about Roark are good guides. Indeed, those feelings are the unarticulated expression of something that *can* be articulated and defended at length, and finally are. Yet without these emotional responses and connections the novel would fail, for perhaps one way of distinguishing a novel from a philosophic treatise is to say that with the novel one must love the truth before one understands it, whereas with the philosophical treatise one must understand the truth before one can love it.

Dominique's emotional reactions to Roark and to the world, however, could not have been simply positive. Rand's optimism about the triumph of goodness would have seemed Pollyannaish if not set off by Dominique's extreme pessimism and conduct. As we have seen, therefore, Rand's problem was to use the literary device of emotional tension without sacrificing her values or her optimism. She solves the problem by giving Dominique a project of destruction in the name of the values for which the book stands. The solution works if we are willing to go along with Rand's literary romanticism, which does not require that characters be exactly true to life to be effective. The device also works because it is possible to see Dominique's actions as Rand's tribute to the reader.

Rand supposes that the reader shares her basic values and sense of life. That supposition can help explain why her books can be so polarizing to readers—either they see it her way or they don't. If the reader does share something of Rand's values, then it is hard to imagine—especially at the time the novel was written—that he or she would not feel some discouragement over the state of the world. Dominique would, therefore, be the hyperbolic literary expression of that discouragement. Moreover, like Dominique the reader would need an alternative vision as encouragement and would need to be persuaded that all was not hopeless, that individual action finally can make a difference. We (the reader) manage to gain the vision and receive the encouragement through Dominique.

The idea of Dominique as the reader would appear to stumble over the fact that no reader, even if in the position to do so, would take such extreme actions as hers, especially toward a lover. But whether part of Rand's conscious intention or not, Dominique's extremism actually buoys the reader's own possibilities for optimism. Rand's tribute that the reader shares her values is coupled with the idea that we will think of Dominique, "You don't really need to go that far" or "It's not as bad or hopeless as all that." This puts the reader in the position of having to travel less distance to get to the main point of the book than does Dominique herself, while still sharing her basic values. Although Dominique must bring herself back from the depths of despair, we (the reader) can start from a relatively more optimistic vantage point in realizing that we need not despair.

This process reinforces other values besides optimism. Dominique is in danger of losing herself—dare we say becoming "selfless"?—in her destructive quest. The work she does in the novel is meaningful in its contribution to destruction, but it is not the sort of work that defines her character as the work of Roark, and even Wynand, does theirs. Consequently the values of self-respect, integrity, productive work, and the like are easier to recognize in ourselves when they are set against someone who both embodies them but is seeking to destroy them. Through this process the reader is again prone to receiving the message about the importance of such values, because he or she sees his or her own proximity to them relative to Dominique's actions.

Finally, it should be noted that Dominique is, in some respects, a person divided against herself. On the one hand she is drawn toward excellence, while on the other she seeks to destroy it. We discussed in chapter 4 as part of Rand's socratic philosophy the importance of character development and some of the ideas connected with it, such as integrity. If we see integrity as wholeness of character, then one of Dominique's achievements at the end of the novel is integrity. She eventually pieces the parts together and becomes whole; her tensions and divisions disappear. We witness the results of this transformation when Dominique has finally come over to Roark.

> [S]he looked up at him and smiled, she knew that she could not have reached this white serenity except as the sum of all the colors, of all the violence she had known. "Howard ... willingly, completely, and always ... without reservations, without fear of anything they can do to you or me ... in any way you wish ... as your wife or your mistress, secretly or openly ... here, or in a furnished room I'll take in some town near a jail where I'll see you through a wire net ... it won't matter.... Howard, if you win the trial—even that won't matter too much. You've won long ago.... I'll remain what I am, and I'll remain with you—now and ever—in any way you want." (699)

Dominique's "white serenity" is not just in keeping with a movement toward her perfection of character but is also expressive of our feeling as we finish the story. We too are made whole at the end, and we feel that wholeness through Dominique. Dominique is the only character in this novel who could make us feel as much, because the others are in some sense either already whole or lost to integrity. We are perhaps pleased and satisfied that Roark at the end is finally getting what he deserves, but we are not thereby ourselves reconciled by his success, because he was not ever divided against himself. We thus experience our own wholeness and sense of completion when Dominique experiences hers.

Dominique, then, is, in the last analysis, both the reader and Rand's tribute to the reader. In the latter case, if Dominique is Rand in a bad mood, then she is also what the reader might become in a bad mood. But as I have just suggested, the reader does not go all the way with Dominique, which has the effect of reinforcing the values Rand wishes to emphasize. If we must criticize Dominique it is not because she inhibits the workings of this novel or fails to relate to the reader. Quite the contrary in both cases. The problem is rather that when compared, for example, to Dagny Taggert of *Atlas Shrugged,* she is little else in this novel but Roark's lover and destroyer. Unlike Dagny, whom we see in a full independent productive role and with a personal past and a future, Dominique lacks a certain development as a whole person. Perhaps Rand did not fill her in because Dominique is closer to Rand than Rand would have liked to admit. When asked by a fan whether Dominique was her embodiment, Rand only denied being as beautiful.[10] Such speculations, however, divert us from the main point. Though Dominique may not be beyond criticism as a character, she does function more successfully in this novel than has sometimes been claimed.

It would seem that a chapter on Dominique would have to discuss the famous "rape" scene before closing. That scene, however, is more appropriate to the topic of the next chapter. We can note in general here, however, that for Rand sexuality is an important feature of the literary character of this novel. In its day, the sex scenes were relatively steamy for a so-called popular novel. The scenes were not included for erotic titillation or to stimulate sales, however, but to express two main ideas: integrity means wholeness of the *whole* person—mind and body both—and consequently, sexuality is an expression of one's deepest values, not a mere physical experience. Indeed, the intensity of passion between Roark and Dominique is meant to signify emotionally a concordance of basic values, not great lustfulness. The point then is to identify us as physical beings, but ones whose physical nature is pervaded by values. Sexuality is perhaps the best way to make that sort of point.

7

Sympathy and Judgment

Readers often think that a novel should be judged by whether one can sympathetically enter into the lives and actions of its characters. We might say, for example, that a character is "wooden," "one dimensional," "aloof," "standoffish," or "undeveloped." These sorts of comments may indicate an inability to sympathize with a character. Interestingly, all such comments have been made about many of Ayn Rand's fictional characters.

Ayn Rand poses some special problems for the reader, for it is not always clear that we actually *do* sympathize with her characters in any normal way. Indeed, if we go back to one of the early accounts of sympathy, namely Adam Smith's, it might even appear that sympathy is something antithetical to Rand. Smith says of sympathy:

> Nothing pleases us more than to observe in other men a fellow-feeling with all the emotions of our own breast; nor are we ever so much shocked as by the appearance of the contrary. . . . Nature, when she formed man for society, endowed him with an original desire to please, and an original aversion to offend his brethren. She taught him to feel pleasure in their favourable, and pain in their unfavourable regard. She rendered their approbation most

flattering and most agreeable to him for its own sake; and their disapprobation most mortifying and most offensive.[1]

What seems most typical of Rand's heroic characters is precisely their *unwillingness* to meet other people halfway or to be moved primarily by the thought of the approbation of others. Rand's individualism appears opposed to the social perspective offered by Smith and perhaps implied by sympathy itself. It would seem, therefore, that Rand's characters would not be the sort with whom one might readily sympathize.

But something is wrong with the foregoing argument. Millions of copies of Rand's fiction have been sold over the years, so readers' failure to sympathize with her characters seems unlikely. We must clarify, then, whether and how these characters fit into a standard form of sympathetic identification and whether any failures of such identification constitute a problem for the novel as a work of fiction.

Failure to sympathize is not necessarily a problem. Literary theorists have long recognized a certain complication with sympathy that is particularly acute in didactic works of fiction (those designed to teach a moral lesson). The problem is whether what draws the reader's sympathy is helpful or distracting to the message being delivered. An eighteenth-century writer presented one version of an ideal solution—one that indicates the issue as well—by saying that a novel should be

> interspersed with liberal and generous sentiments, perfect in the delineation of characters, representing virtue in the most engaging dress, and vice in the most odious colours, tending to ennoble the passions, to awaken tenderness, sympathy, and love (I mean virtuous love), to soften the finer feelings of the mind, and having for its object some important moral. . . . Novels of this kind insensibly operate on the mind.[2]

How true is this view of *The Fountainhead*? Rand denies that she is writing didactic fiction, claiming that there is a difference between such fiction and great works of art. The latter explore universal themes with the "message" or didactic goal being a consequence of that exploration.[3] The former seek primarily to use a specific moral message to encourage certain types of conduct (e.g., fifteenth- and sixteenth-century "morality plays").

Nevertheless, it is instructive to examine how the reader might be drawn into a theme through the characters of a novel, however universal that theme may be. The universality of a theme does not obviate the reader's need to connect to the theme in appropriate ways. The standards identified earlier by the eighteenth-century writer may be just as applicable to universal themes as to particular moral messages. Rand does, for example, wish to paint vice in the most "odious colours," though it is not equally clear that she depicts virtue in the most *"engaging* dress," as we shall discover momentarily. It seems appropriate, therefore, to examine the ways in which we are and are not drawn to her main characters, and why. We can begin with some of the things that do seem to engage the reader's sympathy.

First, it is not difficult to accept the idea that Roark and his mentor, Henry Cameron, are both the victims of injustice. Their competence is never questioned, so they are hated for the work they love and do well. Cameron, speaking to Roark early in the novel, says:

> "I wouldn't care if you were an exhibitionist who's being different as a stunt, as a lark, just to attract attention to himself. It's a smart racket, to oppose the crowd and amuse it and collect admission to the side show. If you did that, I wouldn't worry. But it's not that. You love your work. God help you, you love it! And that's the curse. That's the brand on your forehead for all of them to see.... The substance of them is hatred for any man who loves his work." (54)

Cameron goes on:

> "Here you are, saying to yourself how grand Old Cameron is, a noble fighter, a martyr to a lost cause, and you'd just love to die on the barricades with me and to eat in dime lunch wagons with me for the rest of your life.... Thirty years of a lost cause, that sounds beautiful, doesn't it? But do you know how many days there are in thirty years?" (55)

Passages such as these already put us on the side of Roark against the world and allow us to sympathize with his cause, if not his character. Moreover, the unfolding of the book further reinforces the point. We resent the obscurity of Cameron's death and the success of people like Peter Keating who make it for reasons other than merit and competence. Cameron and Roark are both underdogs, so despite Cameron's words, there is indeed something beautiful and noble in their fighting for a "lost" cause. Generally, then, Rand gains overall sympathy by dividing the world into the just and unjust, the competent and incompetent, the good and evil. We sense quickly which is which and extend our sympathy to the right side of the issue.

Though the general context of sympathy is as just described, Rand often tries to elicit sympathy by, in effect, deconstructing it and recomposing it in a new form. The technique she uses is to give an ordinary sympathetic response a new meaning, either to elicit a new sort of response or (what is more likely) to generate an act of judgment that tells us not to be too trusting of our first emotional reaction. Consider, for example, Peter Keating's relationship with his mother. Keating is the perfect dutiful son, which, other things being equal, would seem to warrant a positive attitude on our part. Instead, the concerned mother and dutiful son are described in passages like the following:

> [Keating] did not want to hear what she [Keating's mother] thought of this: he knew that his only chance to decide was to make the decision before he heard her. (23)

> He wondered whether he really liked his mother. But she was his mother and this fact was recognized by everybody as meaning automatically that he loved her, and so he took for granted that whatever he felt for her was love. He did not know whether there was any reason why he should respect her judgment. She was his mother; this was supposed to take the place of reasons. (24)

These passages are hardly descriptions of filial love and reverence! Rand here turns what is, in most contexts, a positive thing into something negative. It is used to demonstrate both Peter Keating's dependency on others and his substitution of the opinions of others for his own judgment. The reader is thus disconnected from a usual sympathetic landmark and asked to reevaluate its significance; that is, an appeal is made to the reader's judgment. We are aided, however, by the fact that Keating is not himself a particularly sympathetic character, nor for that matter is his suffocating mother.

The technique is even more pronounced when we think of Toohey. Rand through Toohey disassociates or deconstructs many positive sympathetic landmarks. There is, notoriously, the altering of positive connotations associated with such terms as *altruism, selflessness,* and *equality.* In Toohey's long speech toward the end of the book in which he explains to Keating his basic motivation and goals, we see the power of Rand's technique.

> "Peter, my poor old friend, I'm the most selfless man you've ever known. I have less independence than you, whom I just forced to sell your soul. You've used people at least for the sake of what you could get from them for yourself. I want nothing for myself. I use people for the sake of what I can do to them. It's my only function and satisfaction. I have no private purpose. I want power. I want my world of the future. Let all live for all. Let all sacrifice and none profit. Let all suffer and none enjoy. Let progress stop. Let all stagnate. There's equality in stagnation. All subjugated to the will of all. Universal slavery without even the dignity of a master. Slavery to slavery. A great circle—and a total equality. The world of the future." (668)

Notice how Rand surprises us by having Toohey say that he has no "private purpose" but that he wants power. Living for others is equated with unhappiness, equality with stagnation—that is, the two "positive" terms are linked with things that are negative. The same can be said about related and derivative terms as well. In the following short passage notice how "kindliness" and "compassion" are both turned on themselves:

> [Toohey] smiled. The kindliness of his smile embraced [Peter and Catherine] both. The kindliness was so great that it made their

love seem small and mean, because only something contemptible could evoke such immensity of compassion. (240)

It is possible to use this technique in the opposite direction as well. Consider the following from Dominique's column:

"And there it will stand, as a monument to nothing but the egotism of Mr. Enright and of Mr. Roark.... No other setting could bring out so eloquently the essential insolence of this building. It will rise as a mockery to all the structures of the city and to the men who built them.... The Enright House is bright and bold. So is a feather-boa. It *will* attract attention—but only to the immense audacity of Mr. Roark's conceit." (272)

Here "egotism" and "conceit" have positive connotations because we know they are backed by merit.[4] We also know that Dominique does not consider these things "bad" but is writing this way as part of her project of destruction.

Since justice and merit engage the reader's sympathies, Rand does anchor the other terms she wishes to deconstruct in something people ordinarily relate to. Moreover, it is quite necessary, for example, that Toohey be a powermonger, Keating a mediocrity, and Roark extremely competent. If Toohey were a sincerely benevolent person, Keating a competent albeit ambitious man, and Roark less than excellent but with the right values, our sympathies might be mixed. In this Rand follows the prescription of the eighteenth-century writer mentioned earlier. Rand cannot allow us to be too ambivalent, because she wishes us to *think* about certain key concepts. Is it really so bad after all, for example, to consider oneself first? Do collectivities make the marginal difference in moving society forward? Should we trust everyone who speaks of doing things for others?

We can, by contrast, question how successful Rand really is in some of her deconstructions. An indicative but rather minor example comes in Rand's deconstruction of humor. Although the novel opens with Roark laughing, it is a laughter of contempt, not humor. About humor we find passages such as: "[H]ave you noticed that the imbecile always smiles? Man's first frown is the first touch of God on his fore-head" (668). Now we know what Rand is getting at here. People must have serious intent to succeed, and not everything is or should be amusing. But it is simply false to suggest that frowning is the visible precursor to excellence, and it is just as likely that the fulfilled, successful person will always smile as it is that the imbecile will (and further, imbeciles *don't* always smile). The effort to deconstruct smiling or humor to make a point about serious intent is, then, not very successful on one level. Indeed, there would be reason to worry about persons for whom this device *was* successful, since their life might be rather less pleasant than it otherwise needs to be!

Perhaps the most notorious example of readers having trouble sympathizing with the characters in the text is the famous "rape" scene. Rand herself considered rape to be "committing a dreadful crime."[5] It is also quite obvious from the text that Roark's taking of Dominique is no rape:

> One gesture of tenderness from him—and she would have remained cold, untouched by the thing done to her body. But the act of a master taking shameful, contemptuous possession of her was the kind of rapture she had wanted.... She knew that she would not take a bath. She knew that she wanted to keep the feeling of his body, the traces of his body on hers, knowing also what such a desire implied.... They had united in an understanding beyond the violence, beyond the deliberate obscenity of his action; had she meant less to him, he would not have taken her as he did; had he meant less to her, she would not have fought so desperately. The unrepeatable exaltation was in knowing that they both understood this. (220, 221)

As Rand herself later said, "[I]f it's rape—it's rape by engraved invitation." Moreover, in a novel we allow a certain idealization of action to make a point. The problem here is, what is the point?

In this section of the novel we are confronted with remarks like the following:

> It was an act that could be performed in tenderness, as a seal of love, or in contempt, as a symbol of humiliation and conquest. It

could be the act of a lover or the act of a soldier violating an enemy woman. He did it as an act of scorn. Not as love, but as defilement. And this made her lie still and submit. One gesture of tenderness from him . . . (220)

Although it may be clear that Dominique was willing, it is a bit difficult to enter into an act of scorn, defilement, and submission devoid of tenderness. We could perhaps excuse it here if we saw some tenderness elsewhere in the book, but there is remarkably little of it in anyone's love affair. Roark and Dominique do exhibit tenderness sometimes during "pillow talk," and Wynand does for Dominique, as does Roark for Mallory when the latter is at his lowest. But the sexual act—which Rand wants to use as a symbol of love between the self-sufficient—is largely devoid of it.

Not only is it unlikely that the sexual act could continue to downplay tenderness between two who actually love each other, but there is the further problem that Rand may be being simply idiosyncratic as well as inconsistent. The scene may be idiosyncratic because it seems to be more Rand's idea of romance than ours, and the scene may be inconsistent because it is hard to see how the act could be both one of "humiliation" and "scorn" (and thus part of the project of self-destruction) and also one in which Dominique's pleasure indicates what she values most. If humiliation is what she wanted, Peter Keating seems a better match. Roark is best for the right sort of values, but then why the scorn and humiliation? The answer to the latter problem would again seem to be ignorance—Dominique *thinks* she's fulfilling her mission of destruction when in fact she's responding to her deepest values.

But could someone like Dominique not know that the pleasure she feels would have to be in response to some real value? Rand believed that "the highly sexed person is extremely selective. He, or she, can respond only to a special and great attraction. The lesser ones will have no effect on him. . . . It is the same difference between a gourmet and a glutton. Which one of the two has the higher sense of food?"[6] Even ignoring that issue, it is clear that selectivity does not necessarily imply a lack of tenderness. It is almost as if such tenderness would show a sign of weakness and humanity in her characters—a highly arguable attitude to say the least. For better or worse, Rand's heroic characters are largely devoid of the "human" touch that might engender the reader's sympathy. One is still left, however, with the question of why such qualities need to be removed. Couldn't Rand, as our eighteenth-century critic recommends, combine the qualities of both humanity and virtuous heroism?

To answer this question we might want to distinguish between aspirational and connective sympathy. The former concerns the sort of qualities to which one might aspire—in Roark's case, these include independence, integrity, merit, hard work, perseverance, and dedication. We can sympathize with Roark aspirationally because we either do or know we should aspire to such virtues ourselves. We thus readily identify with what it takes to possess these virtues and to act on them. Elements of connective sympathy, by contrast, are qualities that endear people to each other. These might include friendliness, consideration, concern for others, a sense of humor, and the ability to empathize. Roark does not offer us many of these connective hooks, nor do many of Rand's other heroes and heroines for that matter. In this respect, virtue is not put in the most "engaging dress."

Rand herself may well have believed that virtue and the qualities of connective sympathy were incompatible, but whatever her own beliefs, there are some very solid reasons for her divorcing the two in her literature. We must recall, first of all, that one of Rand's purposes is to undermine the credibility of altruism. That would be a difficult task to accomplish in a literary way if altruism were allowed to retain its close association with the elements of connective sympathy mentioned earlier. As we have noticed, Rand must deconstruct some of these elements so that we can see another, less attractive side of altruism—a side that stands in the way of the virtues she wishes to promote.

Second, and in a related way, Rand wishes us to *think* about certain issues rather than simply to *feel* them. The problem that literary theorists have recognized with the technique of sympathy is that it may distract one from the use of the mind by a substitution of feeling. To give her heroes and heroines too many connective hooks would impede the reader's effort to *understand* what the characters are about. The reader might fail to grasp that the virtues exhibited by Roark are the central ones and that the mind is more critical to our humanity than our emotions. It is clear that to attempt to make such points primarily by engaging the reader's sentiments could be counterproductive.

Finally, Rand very well may have seen modern society as largely *corrupted* by these connective elements of sympathy. Those elements are, as the *Banner* clearly testifies, easily subject to a kind of base sentimentality. We might recall in this connection just what the *Banner* appeals to:

> The public asked for crime, scandal and sentiment. Gail Wynand provided it. He gave people what they wanted, plus a justification for indulging the tastes of which they had been ashamed. . . . The *Banner* led great, brave crusades—on issues that had no opposition. It exposed politicians—one step ahead of the Grand Jury; it attacked monopolies—in the name of the downtrodden; it mocked the rich and the successful—in the manner of those who could never be either. . . . The *Banner* was permitted to strain truth, taste and credibility, but not its readers' brain power. (424)

We see from this illustration that modern society is essentially awash in emotion and sentiment. Although perhaps not one of the novel's commonly touted themes, the sentimentality of modern life is undoubtedly indicative for Rand of the more philosophical errors she wishes to identify. If nothing else, a world so dominated by sentiment is likely to lose sight of the primary importance of conceptualization and the mind. To draw us away from that error, then, Rand may need to set her heroes and heroines in opposition to sentiment. The message of the primacy of reason would likely have carried to only the most insightful few had Rand begun with ordinary sentiments and then sought to distinguish their appropriate connection to reason from their inappropriate one. The only feasible alternative was to break cleanly with ordinary sentiments. Perhaps because of Rand's work, we might now be in a better position to integrate more adequately the connective and aspirational elements of sympathy. If nothing else, we certainly learn that the connective qualities need not always side with goodness and virtue.

Given that the *Banner* is the paper of the "masses," it is important here not to draw a pessimistic conclusion about the "average" person. That too would be to give in to the very sentimentality we are here criticizing. However negative some of Rand's major heroes and heroines may sound about "the masses," in this novel, it is the ordinary person who finally votes "not guilty" at Roark's trial. Rand seems to have had a fundamental faith in the basic sense of justice and the humanity of the ordinary person. Though ordinary people may be subject to sentimental asides, Rand treats them with more respect than, for example, she does intellectuals. In *The Fountainhead* especially, virtually all the gatherings of intellectuals are for purposes in line with Toohey's own. Imagine what the verdict on Roark would have been had the jury been composed of people like Lois Cook, Jules Fougler, and Gus Webb! These are individuals who, in their own ways, no longer possess the elemental components of independent judgment, love of excellence, and justice that constitute the building blocks of human existence for Rand.

We have, in a way, come full circle. It was a sense of justice that drew us in to Rand's heroes and heroines, and it is a sense of justice that causes the characters to sympathize with each other. It is that sense that binds together the heroes and heroines and its lack that unites the villains. It is also justice that brings us into the book and that connects someone like Roark to the ordinary person in the novel. Moreover, of the connective elements of sympathy, it is perhaps the passion for justice that the novel as a whole most engages.

Rand's literary devices with respect to appeals (or lack thereof) to sentiment and sympathy may all, therefore, have legitimate and plausible bases given her purposes and in light of the context in which she wrote. But there is another device Rand uses, or rather relies on, in her efforts to engage the reader, and for Rand this factor is of critical importance. It is what she calls a "sense of life." Rand states that "a sense of life is a pre-conceptual equivalent of metaphysics, an emotional, subconsciously integrated appraisal of man and of existence."[7] Since art "is a selective re-creation of reality according to an artist's metaphysical value-judgments,"[8] artists are projecting a metaphysics through the sense of life portrayed by their art. The process means that "art brings man's concepts to the perceptual level of his consciousness and allows him to grasp them directly, as if they were percepts."[9]

The idea of a "sense of life" and its connection to art is one of the most insightful and intriguing of Rand's philosophical notions. It is also one of the more problematic as a literary device for her in particular. Is there not something odd, distorting, and thus fundamentally risky about presenting the conceptual (that is, the abstract and intellectual) perceptually (in this case in terms of feelings or emotions) when one sees the problem of modern life as being one of too much reliance on the perceptual? Can one, in other words, even begin to appreciate the nature of the conceptual if it is reduced to, or expressed in terms of, the perceptual? The projection of the conceptual by means of the perceptual is especially delicate if art is supposed to be "addressed to the conceptual level of man's consciousness,"[10] for one is always in danger of not reaching that level. Indeed, treating the conceptual perceptually is just another version of the "moral hazard" identified in the eighteenth century when considering how the sentiments might mislead in the promotion of virtue, because virtue may be critically dependent on factors that are not sentimental.

Rand tells us that art salutes rather than justifies our sense of life.[11] But one salutes what is already completed and accomplished, suggesting that either one shares the right sense of life for appreciating Rand's works or one does not. Those who do not are apparently lost to Rand, but even those who do share her sense of life, but who may not have articulated all its elements, are moved no closer to a conceptual comprehension if all they are receiving is a salute. What is missing are the developmental or procedural aspects that go into making up a "sense of life" or a conceptual framework.

Consider in this connection that we see very few signs of intellectual development in Rand's heroes. Roark, for example, does not draw conclusions so much as he pronounces them. The most extreme case is John Galt of *Atlas Shrugged*. These characters make philosophical speeches throughout the novels, but we see none of the reasoning that went into their conclusions—only the logical connections that are part of them. That is to say, since the characters do not make errors, explore issues, follow a wrong lead, get refuted, struggle with philosophical problems, or gain new insights, the *process* of intellection is essentially ignored. But it is this very process that is needed to help the reader understand how the conceptual differs from the perceptual and also to lead the reader *from* the perceptual *to* the conceptual. Without these procedural guides, these heroes stand high above us on a platform—with the ladder pulled up. We are undoubtedly filled with awe and admiration, but it is not clear how we are to get on the platform ourselves. And in this respect, the effect may be exactly the opposite of what Rand should want—namely, we are left more with a sentiment (admiration) than with any comprehension of the nature of the conceptual.

Rand perhaps tries to make up for the problem precisely by using long, philosophical speeches, and this surely provides *some* idea of how the conceptual may be appropriately used. But the speeches are either disconnected from the perceptual by being examples of pure conceptual abstraction or they end up (apparently by Rand's own view of art) being part of a *perceptual* appeal. Consequently, it is not clear how effective the speeches are in actually moving the reader not already adept at philosophy beyond the perceptual.[12] It is conceivable that the reader may be drawn *away* from philosophy, thinking all the philosophizing has been done in the speeches themselves. In any case, our witnessing some of the heroes and heroines' developmental movement toward certain conclusions need not diminish them. We do not, for example, think any less of Elizabeth Bennet in Austen's *Pride and Prejudice* when we watch her discover the roots of her own prejudice. Dominique is, as we have seen, the one who comes closest in this novel to exhibiting development, but Dominique is more often struggling with a mood than growing intellectually.

It is ironic, and perhaps not unrelated to this very issue, that Rand has been accused of engendering sycophants rather than attracting persons who exhibit the very qualities of independence and critical judgment she advocates. Of course, Rand is not responsible for the failings of her admirers, but she may not have fully appreciated the dimensions of the problem we are discussing in relationship to her readers. At one point, while defending the benefits of art perceptualizing the conceptual, Rand related how readers of *The Fountainhead* told her that they solved moral dilemmas by imagining what Howard Roark would do in a certain situation: "[T]he image of Roark gave them the answer. They sensed, almost instantly, what he would or would not do."[13] But isn't it just as important here not only to be able to imagine what Roark would do but to know *why* he would do it?

The "moral hazard" of Rand's art that we have just identified needs to be tempered with the recognition that *The Fountainhead* has been thought of as a philosophical novel—that is, a novel about ideas—since its inception. In that respect, Rand has not at all failed to bring the reader to at least the recognition of the importance of ideas and concepts to her art and to human existence generally. Nothing discussed thus far should undermine the tremendous magnitude of that achievement.

8

Individualism

If nothing else, *The Fountainhead* is a novel that depicts the meaning of individualism. Although we have discussed this theme in various ways in earlier chapters, its importance makes it worthy of separate treatment. Yet since the theme of individualism *is* so pervasive in this novel, we also need a way to focus the discussion here. Roark's speech at the end of the novel (709–17) would seem to be a natural focal point. In addition, we have two promises to keep, made at the end of chapter 5—namely, to say something about why Roark would do Keating's work for him and to comment on Rand's optimism in light of the pessimism in the opening paragraph of Roark's speech. The latter issue comes up as a matter of course in dealing with Roark's speech. At that point we will find ourselves confronting the former issue as well.

In her book *For the New Intellectual,* which collects the main speeches and passages of Rand's novels, Rand leaves off the few paragraphs describing the audience that come just before Roark's speech. These paragraphs are, however, quite significant to understanding the speech, especially if Rand's art means to distill into an emotion a complex abstraction. In these introductory paragraphs, Roark is described as "a man totally innocent of fear"(709). The audience too, though not innocently, is momentarily free of fear: "[T]hey felt [Roark] had no chance. They could drop the nameless resentment, the sense of insecurity which he aroused in most people." The key term in these introductory paragraphs may be, therefore, *innocence*—a term used also in the third of the three paragraphs, in which Roark is said to stand before the audience "in the innocence of his own mind." What exactly is Roark innocent of? In one way the answer is easy: Roark has never known the emotions named in the second paragraph, fear, need, dependence, and hatred. But why exactly is he innocent of these things?

The answer to this last question will force us to realize that individualism for Rand is more than the social or political doctrine for which she is best known; rather, it is a state of character or an approach to life. Roark's speech indiscriminately mixes these distinct senses of individualism, because Rand sees them as inextricably connected. But historically the social and political idea of allowing the individual to act on his or her own choices without control by the community or a higher authority has not necessarily been linked to a particular form of character or way of living. Indeed, some might argue that the idea of individual social freedom could even be inconsistent with the idea of a "right way to be." In Rand's case, however, the reverse holds. It is clearly the "right way to be" that is to give us our sense of why individual liberty is so important.

It can be said that Roark is innocent because he has never allowed himself to be corrupted. If this is our sense of *innocent,* then to be innocent of fear would not mean being incapable of it, or even being without it, but rather never having been corrupted by it (or having had it mark one's corruption). To be corrupted by an emotion, one would have to substitute it for one's judgment with respect to some action or goal. We might do such things because of peer pressure, a desire to conform, a need for approval, sentiment, or fear itself. It is not that all such feelings are necessarily bad, but they would become so if they were substituted for using the mind. If the members of the audience had surrendered their judgment to someone or something else, a nameless resentment toward one who had not so surrendered might develop. Consequently, a fear of one who possesses the strength not to give in would be a natural accompaniment to that resentment. Roark is certainly innocent of this sort of fear or resentment.

The same point can be made about Roark's innocence of mind, since innocence of mind is simply the precondition for innocence of fear. Roark is innocent of mind because he has never surrendered it to anything else. This point is, of course, just another way of referring to the absence of being a second-hander. Those in the audience (the reader?) are presumably not so innocent in these ways.

> [T]hey remembered the misery of the moments when, in loneliness, a man thinks of the bright words he could have said, but had not found, and hates those who robbed him of the courage. The misery of knowing how strong and able one is in one's own mind, the radiant picture never to be made real. (709)

Roark was never "robbed," nor did he lack strength and ability in his own mind. He thus grew to know no fear, just as others may grow to know it.

Although it appears a strange question, it is still worth asking at this point what is so wrong with being ruled by fear (or the other negative emotions mentioned). Two answers jump immediately to mind, neither of which applies to Roark. The first is that these emotions are unpleasant to experience. The second is that these emotions lead to social conflict or disharmony of some sort. These reasons need not be rejected altogether, but to understand the sort of individualism Roark represents, we must understand that the problem with these emotions stems from their tendency to undermine self-sufficiency and active living, not their inherent unpleasantness or their social effects. We have noted elsewhere that Rand believed reason and judgment should guide our actions. The novel thus depicts those guided by their own conclusions versus those in the grips of the opinions and attitudes of others, or even in the grips of their own emotions. It is tempting to stop here and simply draw the line between the individualist and the nonindividualist on the basis of the independence of one's judgment. Doing so, however, would cause us to miss the point of Roark's speech, which is to connect independence with human advancement or successful living, and not just to distinguish between the individualist and the second-hander.

In an article written for *Reader's Digest* not long after the publication of *The Fountainhead,* Rand discusses the moral basis of individualism in terms of the "active" and the "passive man."[1] The "active man" is the originator, the producer, and the achiever. That person needs independence in order to think and work. The "passive man" by contrast welcomes the chance to escape the responsibility to use his mind. One is passive insofar as one is in the grips of something else, be it an emotion, blind devotion, the opinions of others, a tradition, a custom, a habit, or a momentary whim. One may be engaged in activities when passive, but one is not *active* when what one is doing does not stem from self-initiated choices, which can come only from the unconstrained use of one's mind and judgment.

The great philosopher Spinoza—who also divided people into the active and free versus the passive and slavish—once said, "[A] free man thinks of nothing less than death, and his wisdom is not a meditation upon death but upon life."[2] In many respects this idea sums up the principle behind Roark's speech and Rand's view of individualism. Indeed, similar phrases appear in Roark's speech: "[T]he creator is not concerned with disease, but with life"; "[T]he choice is independence or dependence.... This is the basic issue. It rests upon the alternative of life or death" (713). The principle here is the integral triadic connection between activity, life, and independence. It is opposed to the connection that exists between passivity, death, and subservience. To be active is the free person's meditation on what is needed to advance life, and the advancement of life comes from those who are active and free. Indeed, freedom and activity become virtually one in the sense that both are manifestations of directedness toward the self rather than toward others. As Roark puts it in his speech, such an individual is "self-sufficient, self-motivated, self-generated. A first cause, a fount of energy, a life force, a Prime Mover" (711). Passivity, by contrast, is a form of self-immolation and ultimately death. Consequently, when one is focused on what promotes life one is *being active*. Since the mind is the tool by which we comprehend and deal with the world around us ("his brain is his only weapon," 711), we can advance life only by using our minds. It is the independent use of the mind, therefore, that defines activity and thus ultimately individualism.

The opening three paragraphs of Roark's speech—the first of which we cited in chapter 5—all speak to independence of mind. The creator and innovator or discoverer are individuals who did not rely on what others thought or believed but followed their own ideas and insights: "[T]heir goals differed, but they all had this in common: that the step was first, the road new, the vision unborrowed" (710). All the benefits we have received—that is, all the things that enhance human living—came from those whose "step was first." The individualist, then, is one who seeks independence for its own sake.

> His truth was his only motive. His own truth, and his own work, to achieve it in his own way.... The creation, not its users. The creation, not the benefits others derived from it. The creation which gave form to his truth. He held his truth above all things and against all men. (710–11)

And the reason, as we learn early on in the speech, that independence is so critical is that only an individual can think: "the primary act—the process of reason—must be performed by each man alone" (711).

But Rand (through Roark) is equally insistent that "no creator was prompted by a desire to serve his brothers." From the point of view of the novel, Rand *must* hold that the welfare of others is not the creator's motivation; otherwise it would seem possible to argue that service to humanity is what justifies creative acts or that one should be moved to the creative by the desire for such service. That position could in turn mean that Roark would not be justified in bombing Cortlandt and should be found guilty. In any case, in light of what is said in the opening paragraphs of the speech, it would in fact be *irrational* to act for the sake of one's "brothers," because "every great new thought was opposed. Every great new invention was denounced." Indeed, innovators are "torn on the rack," "condemned to suffer," subjected to "hatred," and thought "sinful" (710); they are "denied, opposed, persecuted, [and] exploited" (715), abused, frustrated, and lonely (717).

We come now to discuss Rand's optimism and even to a question about individualism itself. Why is Rand optimistic in the face of the treatment the individualist will most certainly receive? More troubling still, why would the creative individual—given that that individual is not moved by the future benefit of mankind—wish to undergo negative treatment and perhaps leave all the benefits of one's ideas only to future generations? Rand's answer to this last question may very well be her later novel *Atlas Shrugged,* in which apparently the response is "he wouldn't." But if he wouldn't, why does he so stubbornly continue to create and innovate in the face of such treatment? Even in *Atlas Shrugged* a number of the main characters persevere rather than resign from the world.

There are three levels at which the optimism question can be answered—the literal, the personal, and the metaphysical. The first and literalist reading says that life will simply not continue, or at best will stagnate, if the innovators are missing. Since life seems to go on, what these individuals have to offer eventually comes to play a role and make a difference. The literalist reading is certainly a form of optimism and perhaps explains the progress of the human species, but it does not speak to the question of individual motivation, which must have no such concern as the progress of the species. Moreover, such a reading is not much comfort to those noninnovators who might otherwise gain were their benefits not deferred as the creative ones are subjected to ill treatment.

It would seem, then, that the reasons for optimism would have to fall in the "personal" category to explain individual motivation. This is stated simply by Roark well before his speech (and ironically, to Peter Keating):

> "Peter, before you can do things for people, you must be the kind
> of man who can get things done. But to get things done, you must
> love the doing, not the secondary consequences. The work, not
> the people. Your own action, not any possible object of your char-
> ity." (604)

One continues to work, therefore, because of the love of doing the work. This not only explains why the individualist will put up with abuse, but also perhaps why Roark might do Keating's work for him—for the love of the doing. Indeed, Roark tells us as much when he agrees to design Cortlandt: "[T]he only thing that matters, my goal, my reward, my beginning, my end is the work itself" (605). Roark will not get the work any other way, so he makes the agreement.

But does this really answer our question, or does it only raise new ones? Why would Roark compromise what must certainly be a general principle not to allow second-handers to be countenanced? Why doesn't he wait for a later opportunity to work on low-income housing? He was willing to wait for all his other projects, so it cannot be the pain of waiting that compels him now. And would not allowing someone else to take the credit for one's work be every bit as much a compromise of integrity as allowing one's plans to be altered? For even though the object exists and one can take some private satisfaction from that, its existence under false pretenses suggests that the way these innovative creations come about is through the likes of Peter Keating—a posture surely more threatening to one's future work and principles than succumbing to cosmetic changes by a corporate board. Finally, this is not the first time Roark has done Keating's work. He has done so since college. The Cortlandt project is, from what we can tell from the novel, the *most* excusable of all these acts. The other substitutions seem much less justifiable, more irrational, and may, in fact, contribute to Keating's own demise. What, then, can explain them?

In answering the last question, one is perhaps pushed to make conjectures that may be less than obvious. I believe that much of the answer, even regarding the novel as a whole, is found in the following passage, which comes not far before Roark's speech:

> [Roark] did not know that Wynand had once said all love is exception-making; and Wynand would not know that Roark had loved him enough to make his greatest exception, one moment when he tried to compromise. Then he knew it was useless, like all sacrifices. (699)

Could Roark's *love* of his work explain, if it does not justify, the exception of helping Keating, just as it moved him to exception in Wynand's case? And although the consequences are much the same in both cases, we have already noted that consequences do not matter much, especially, we might add, to lovers. Lovers are compelled by the object of their love to the point of ignoring consequences that others would regard as normal and rational considerations. And in many significant respects the protagonists of this novel are lovers in this way, while the villains are not. Roark makes the exceptions noted; Mallory makes exceptions to the principles of civil order when he shoots at Toohey; Wynand makes numerous exceptions to his usual habits for both Roark and Dominique; Dominique marries men she does not love for the sake of the one she does; Henry Cameron's exception— the reverse of Dominique's—involves hiring Roark though he believes the world will destroy him; and if we look at Roark's early commissions from people like Austin Heller we notice other exceptions (e.g., ignoring the wishes of corporate boards) from the standard ways people do business.

Some of the exceptions are to standard practices, others to rules, principles, or attitudes that might otherwise govern. All the exceptions, however, have love in common, and it is the same sort of love— the love of the good or the best. The lover of the good or the best is compelled as much, or even more, by what ought to be as by what is. Roark's buildings ought to exist and his genius be appreciated. People ought to be moved by integrity and a desire for excellence instead of by second-handedness and mediocrity. People ought to love one another for qualities of character rather than prestige. In a significant way, then, all the innovations and creations Roark mentions in his speech are "exceptions," for they move us from what is to what ought to be, and what ought to be is not what is ordinarily the case.

The exceptional quality of love is fueled by its passionate nature. Despite all the talk of the mind, reason, and judgment, what is equally striking about Rand's characters is their passion. The main characters pursue their goals with relentless dedication and purpose, and the novel as a whole—as sales and controversy about Rand's ideas indicate—produces extraordinary passions in the reader. Indeed, one might justifiably conclude that while this novel may be about a certain conception of individualism, its object is love: to produce in the reader a love of the good and of those who advance it, or at least to force the reader to confront that love in his or her own case.

We come, consequently, to our third meaning of optimism, Rand's metaphysical or deep optimism. This form of optimism might be described as the harmony of the previous two. As it turns out, what ultimately gives an individual the greatest and most meaningful satisfaction, what is most in line with personal integrity, what most accords with individualism, is also what advances humankind in general. In Rand's later nonfiction writing, she called this the "benevolent universe" premise. The universe is suited to personal excellence. One does not act out of step with the natural order when one is active in the sense just described; rather, one furthers or harmonizes with it. Ultimately, then, the universe is not tragic. What is good is not alienated from the order of the universe such that it succumbs to isolated defeat. Rather, the reverse is true. The true order of things is reflected in examples of the good or the best. This perspective is truly optimistic, because it says that personal success and achievement are not only in harmony with the natural order of things but represent their very meaning. We must, of course, keep in mind that this optimism is to be understood in light of the general framework described in chapter 4. That is to say that although "the world [may be] perishing from an orgy of self-sacrifice" (717)—as Roark puts it in his speech—we may still hold to the optimism just described. That optimism expresses what is inherent and essential in the nature of things and thus ought to be, even if it is not "normal" in the sense of being statistically predominate at the moment. Indeed, the inevitability idea may be an expression of the natural tendency of the two (personal and social) to harmonize.

Another deep feature of Rand's metaphysical optimism is her view, discussed in chapter 5, of the ultimate impotence of evil. We left the problem open ended in that chapter and shall continue to leave it so here. But one can see the optimism her view of evil exhibits, for surely one way of interpreting our opening query about the inevitability of the good is to see that Rand believes that evil is impotent in the face of good. She is explicit about this point in *Atlas Shrugged:* "[E]vil, not value, is an absence and a negation, evil is impotent and has no power but that which we let it extort from us" (1024). *The Fountainhead* as a whole can be understood as an expression of this thesis. Roark never gives in, because he knows the power of evil comes from giving in. Moreover, in other places near Roark's speech, the key virtue is expressed in terms of not giving in (e.g., 685, 701). What Dominique (and perhaps Wynand) learns is that one need not buckle in the face of evil, that if one persists it can be overcome. Roark's "lesson" to us is that perseverance pays—not necessarily in the sense of leading to a specific outcome such as a "not guilty" vote or to the recognition one deserves, but in the sense of being in accord with the principle that evil has no power of its own. It has no power, as Toohey well knows, because "the soul ... is that which can't be ruled. It must be broken" (665). The unbroken soul, the person of independence, deprives evil of the power that must be given to it for it to possess power at all. The universe, then, does not have for Rand an intrinsic power of evil, and that is a form of optimism.

How plausible this optimism concerning evil really is shall, as we said, be left open. But we can certainly ask here what would happen if lots of people compromised their power to evil. One who wishes to remain independent under such circumstances could thereby face a daunting force that has all the effects of a positive reality! It would seem, then, that great evil of this sort could be matched only by great goodness (e.g., Roark against Toohey) and not necessarily by the "average" good person. We must remember, however, that *The Fountainhead* is Romantic literature. What is writ large in grandiose characters in principle represents the little opportunities to compromise each of us faces every day.

After establishing the connection between life, activity, and independence of mind, Roark's speech continues with an attack on altruism (712).[3] We have already discussed much of what is said in these paragraphs, but two points are worth mention here. First, and in light of our previous comments about love, the altruist is one who "degrades the dignity of man and ... degrades the conception of love." How does the altruist degrade love? The altruist degrades love by substituting people per se for the good and this ignores *what type* of person they are. To ignore the type of person one is to love is to say it matters little what that person is like, which indifference in turn undermines the good itself. Since love seeks to promote, defend, or advance the object of one's love, it carries with it an inherent dignity or normative quality. Love in effect says, "This is what I value," and thus to be indifferent about the presence of goodness is to degrade it, at least by default. It is not the concern for others to which Roark objects but the *indiscriminate* concern. Hitler and Stalin, to pick two figures from the era of this novel, were "others" too, after all.

The second point worth noting about these paragraphs on altruism is the connection between altruism and conformity. In a manner reminiscent of John Stuart Mill's defense of nonconformity and autonomy in *On Liberty,* we find Roark saying,

> "Men have been taught that it is a virtue to agree with others. But the creator is the man who disagrees. Men have been taught that it is a virtue to swim with the current. But the creator is the man who goes against the current. Men have been taught that it is a virtue to stand together. But the creator is the man who stands alone." (713)

Of course, Roark is undoubtedly referring to *substantive* nonconformity, rather than simple difference (recall our citing in chapter 7 the words of Henry Cameron to Roark on being different). The point to notice here is that if we must live for others, then it is either for others as they are or for others as they can and ought to be. If the latter, then the whole question of the meaning and nature of the good arises all over again, and one would presumably have developed some principles of selection based on the good. If the former, then one's attachment amounts to a commitment to the status quo. Because the group is primary, altruism may be opposed to all forms of nonconformity, but it would certainly be opposed to the substantive. Substantive nonconformity begins by holding that the group's ways or opinions are not one's primary concern. Superficial nonconformity does not require this beginning, only that one finds the margins of what the group will tolerate and then acts accordingly. If the group is primary, even this marginal conduct can be threatened, but it may also be a form of exception that proves the rule.

For Rand, then, human existence in general, and one's own life in particular, is critically dependent on substantive innovation and advancement. In this speech anyway, and for the novel as a whole, the roles of custom, habit, tradition, and patterned activity are deprecated. We may be able to take what is said here at face value and disparage all tradition and custom. Roark's speech lends itself to that reading with its sweeping pronouncements on nonconformity and innovation. A somewhat milder reading would suggest that Rand is dealing with essentials and not every facet of the issue. At the essential level innovation is what is critical to moving life forward, but it does not follow that human existence should be without custom and tradition. Meaningful traditions themselves originally may very well be the result of the work of innovators. In any case, emphasizing innovation would at least mean that one would not want to serve tradition and custom at its expense. And since that is the more likely danger, a focus on innovation is surely warranted.

The section of the speech on altruism gives way to the political portion of the speech (714–16). The central theme of this part of the speech is perhaps summed up in the sentence "[I]n all proper relationships there is no sacrifice of anyone to anyone" (714). The model of trade—in which one person gives value for value to another—is used to describe how individuals who neither demand nor give sacrifices would relate to one another at the social and political levels. And since most often in the past sacrifices have been involuntarily coerced socially, the political conclusion of this section is that "the only good which men can do to one another and the only statement of their proper relationship is—Hands off!" (715). Probably, however, one should refer to *Atlas Shrugged* in general, and the practices of Galt's Gultch (the ideal society described in that novel) in particular, for the fullest treatment of these themes. Here the point is to notice the connection between individualism and the model of trade.

One of the more interesting claims of this section of the speech is the following: "Civilization is the progress toward a society of privacy. The savage's whole existence is public, ruled by the laws of his tribe. Civilization is the process of setting man free from men" (715). If Rand is correct in this assessment, one can only wonder about our own future with its increasing tendency to move every facet of our lives into the public political realm. But the conceptual point is not just to raise further issues about the role of custom and tradition, but also to recognize why this statement would be made. What is private and not rule governed is also the area of personal freedom one possesses. Since "the basic need of the creator is independence" and "the reasoning mind ... demands total independence in function and motive" (712), personal freedom is not just a desirable state but an absolutely central one to all the values here espoused. Thus, as we noted at the opening of this chapter, Rand's political views are derived from of other values and premises.

Yet if Roark can succeed in a world where the realm of personal freedom is not ideal, why should we hold that such freedom is necessary at all? One answer, of course, is that we are not all Howard Roarks, able to stand up to such a world. Another answer might be that to the degree we are unfree, we are deprived of the benefits of Roark-like people. The most plausible answer in light of the positions of this novel would be to say that freedom is a principle required or implied by the other principles we have discussed. The world may deviate from this principle, but doing so threatens the viability of the other principles. One might, for example, be able to be creative in a politically repressive environment, but such an environment is certainly not *encouraging* to creativity; and because it is *in principle* opposed to creativity, the long-term effects will be particularly negative. Roark lives in a predominantly free society, so his obstacles are relatively minor—lack of contracts, and courtroom dramas. We can, however, easily imagine a society (such as Hitler's Germany or Stalin's Russia) in which even the Roarks might be silenced for a while. Rand herself, after all, emigrated. But this again brings us around to Rand's "problem of evil," about which we have said enough.

The final section of the speech has to do with Roark's personal motives for destroying Cortlandt and how what he said in the other sections of the speech concerns that action. For our purposes here, perhaps the most important theme of this closing section is the connection between individualism and responsibility.

> "Why was the building disfigured [by those who altered Roark's original design]? For no reason. Such acts never have any reason, unless it's the vanity of some second-handers who feel they have a right to anyone's property, spiritual or material. Who permitted them to do it? No particular man among the dozens in authority. No one cared to permit it or to stop it. No one was responsible. No one can be held to account. Such is the nature of all collective action." (716)

We see that it is in the nature of collectivism (and by implication altruism) to so disperse responsibility that no one can be identified with it. It is in the nature of collectivism because its primary unit of analysis is the group or society rather than the individual. To assign responsibility to a group or society is to assign it to no one in particular. This is not to say that the individual is avoided altogether. The Tooheys of the world are still "responsible" in the sense of creating the collectivist atmosphere, but part of their strategy—shown with great insight throughout this novel—is to avoid being personally linked in any direct way to particular consequences or results. All consequences are to be tied to the group, and Toohey forms group after group throughout the novel. Moreover, Toohey, we should recall, almost never holds any official position in the organizations he founds or with which he is involved. It is thus especially important that Roark stand up and be identified with the creation and destruction of Cortlandt.

Apart from this speech being a part of this novel and thus having to end with a reference to Roark's own particular case (since he is defending himself and not reading a philosophical paper), responsibility should be seen as the end product of the ideas enumerated in this chapter. If creativity, innovation, and thought can come only from individuals, then it is individuals who should be responsible. And if we reflect on the idea that evil derives its power from, and that survival depends on, creative thought, then individuals *will be* responsible, since there is no one else, by definition, who can be. If the individualist stands alone, it is clear who is connected to an idea or result. Originator and consequence are thus linked without mediation, making individualism and responsibility very much part of the same active process.

It would seem, then, that we could encourage individualism with a system that clearly defined responsibility, and the right to property mentioned in the passage cited would certainly be an element in such a system. We might also want to think of responsibility in moral terms, as something that gives people what they deserve, what is fair or just. To diffuse responsibility is to diffuse morality or justice, since it is less certain who deserves what. Yet while both these reasons are certainly a part of the philosophy expressed in the speech, it is interesting that Roark takes neither approach in defending himself. That is, he neither appeals to the benefits derived from encouraging responsibility nor dwells on the justice of the case (though what is due him is mentioned). Both of these reasons are themselves fundamentally social in character. Rather, Roark appeals to the primacy and sanctity of the individual: "I came here to say that I do not recognize anyone's right to one minute of my life. Nor to any part of my energy. Nor to any achievement of mine. No matter who makes the claim, how large their number or how great their need" (717).

The appeal to the primacy and sanctity of the individual is again an appeal to what is essential or fundamental rather than what is derivative. Social benefits are the consequence of innovation, not the cause: "[I]t is said that I [Roark] have destroyed the home of the destitute. It is forgotten that but for me the destitute *could not* have had this particular *home*" (716, emphasis added). Even moral principles are grounded in (reduced to?) the individualist bedrock: "I recognize no obligations toward men except one: to respect their freedom and to take no part in a slave society" (717).[4] What is deserved or undeserved will itself presumably start from this conception of social obligation, and it is this conception of social obligation that is most consistent with the idea of personal responsibility due to the central place this conception accords individual freedom.

Yet despite our discussions of optimism, we are still left wondering at the end of this speech why the group of people in the courtroom did not do to Roark what he stated in his speech such groups always do to innovators. For to argue that Rand is optimistic is not to show why this audience is likely to be. The answer to this question, and the subject of our very brief concluding chapter, is simply that they are Americans.

9

Conclusion: An American Novel

"The philosophy we need is a conceptual equivalent of America's sense of life."

—Philosophy: Who Needs It?

Although many of us perhaps aspire to write the "great American novel," one way to conclude our interpretation of *The Fountainhead* is to say that this is exactly what Rand has done! It is hard to imagine this novel being written anywhere else or set in any context other than America. One commentator, for example, has correctly noted,

> *The Fountainhead* is a work of American literature; of that we can be sure. And I want to emphasize the word *American*, because it's an adjective that we don't take seriously enough when we talk about *The Fountainhead*. This book is saturated with American experience, with the life of the American city, with the lives of American people pursuing archetypically American occupations—businessman, journalist, builder of skyscrapers. It is filled with the language, the gestures, the strange social customs and improvisations of Americans.[1]

Yet the meaning of the centrality of America is perhaps something of a controversial point in this novel. The aforementioned commentator, after citing the line from Roark's speech that America is "the noblest country in the history of man," also claims that Rand "reimagines" America from a "point that lies *outside* conventional American opinion."[2] That is the perspective Roark is said to take as well.

Although it is true that Rand's original, immigrant status makes her an outsider to America, Roark should not be thought of as reimagining America from the outside so much as *recapturing* it from the inside. Here is the whole passage from which the phrase "the noblest country in the history of men" is taken:

> "Now observe the results of a society built on the principle of individualism. This, our country. The noblest country in the history of men. The country of greatest achievement, greatest prosperity, greatest freedom. This country was not based on selfless service, sacrifice, renunciation or any precept of altruism. It was based on a man's right to the pursuit of happiness. His own happiness. Not anyone's else's. A private, personal, selfish motive. Look at the results. Look into your own conscience." (715)

The intrinsic principles of America are there for us to rediscover at any time. America was built on the principle of individualism, and the jurors are asked to search their consciences for the truth that lies within them. In a novel about essentials, the argument here is that individualism is what is essential to, and at the very core of, America. *That* proposition may be arguable from the outside, but in and of itself it is very much a perspective from the inside.

The jurors acquit Roark not because he convinces them to reimagine America, but rather because he appeals to what they all know America to really be about, deep down inside. Indeed, a "not guilty" verdict would seem rather unlikely if the jurors had been required to reconstruct the American experience to fit what Roark was saying. A hung jury would seem more plausible, since there could be many possible reimaginings of America. That America is not exactly like the vision Roark lays out in his speech is not an argument against this point. As we have stressed repeatedly, the current state of affairs may not be decisive when thinking about the central principles that characterize a person, event, or set of circumstances. The jurors acquit Roark because they are Americans and see that it is American values to which Roark appeals. The speech is successful because it asks the jurors to rediscover their own Americanness. It would be hard to imagine anything other than an American jury being moved by such an argument, because it would be hard to imagine anything but an American jury taking individualism so seriously.

Later in the speech, well after the passage just cited, Roark alludes again to the inherent Americanism of his position when he says, "To my country, I wish to give the ten years which I will spend in jail if my country *exists no longer*" (717, emphasis added). Here we see a recognition of a country drifting away from what it really is. Moreover, there is the implication that America is essentially in accord with the principles Roark identified earlier in the speech. By the time we get to *Atlas Shrugged,* however, America has completely abandoned her essential principles. In that novel America has drifted so far from its individualist roots that the protagonists must abandon it for their own ideal society.

Roark on the other hand, like Socrates before him, appears quite willing to martyr himself and give a substantial portion of his life to America's historical identity. Ten years in jail in the prime of one's life is a lot to give, and Rand did not have to have Roark say he would be willing to do so, unless the principles Roark espouses were not only intrinsic to him, but to America as well. There is the supposition in Roark's statement that Americans in the end will retain their sense of justice, if only they can see through the fog of collectivism and appreciate what has been in them all along. The leading characters in *Atlas Shrugged,* however, have chosen voluntary exile—reminiscent of Aristotle's response to Athens when he was charged with the same "crimes" as Socrates—rather than submit to a thoroughly corrupt order.

There is a form of reimagining that is, nevertheless, different from, though not unrelated to, American individualism. It is quite central to both Roark and America. It is the idea of transformation, the

idea of moving a step beyond where we are now to something greater
and better. We have noted often in this novel the presence of the ideas
of innovation, restructuring, reshaping, and production. There is little
talk of renewal, tradition, or passive enjoyment. We are, in a way,
meant to constantly ascend. That, we should recall, is the image that
closes the book, and it is interesting to note the symbols of the current
status quo that are transcended:

> She saw him standing above her, on the top platform of the
> Wynand Building. He waved to her.
> The line of the ocean cut the sky. The ocean mounted as the
> city descended. She passed the pinnacles of bank buildings. She
> passed the crowns of courthouses. She rose above the spires of
> churches.
> Then there was only the ocean and the sky and the figure of
> Howard Roark. (727)

This single passage simultaneously looks to the essence of America,
prefigures *Atlas Shrugged,* and captures the central spirit of *The Fountainhead.*

Notice how the symbols of a current civilization (banks,
churches, courthouses) are transcended, leaving only the ocean, the
sky, and Roark. America too has been pictured as an open frontier, an
untrammeled space to be reconfigured by the efforts and vision of
those who settle her. Roark stands before all that is wide open, just as
America is said to have unlimited possibilities. The unlimited spaces
symbolize not only possibility but hope and promise as well, not to
mention freedom. These are American symbols and American values
and allow us to read the passage in terms of recapturing them.

Rand's magnum opus, *Atlas Shrugged,* is also foreshadowed
here. In that novel a new society, spearheaded by the novel's heroes
and heroines, rises out of the old. These individuals create out of what
appears to be barren land a new order, one that is defined not just by
its social structure but by new technology as well. Like Roark atop his
girders, the individuals of *Atlas Shrugged* use their innovative technology first to exile themselves, and finally to emerge triumphant over a
decayed social order. Roark's posture above civilization and Dominique's

rise to meet him in the closing sentences allow us to regard *The Fountainhead* as prefiguring *Atlas Shrugged.*

Finally, the closing scene captures the central idea of this novel—namely, individualism. For the image of Roark standing above all else facing only the vastness of sky and ocean gives perfect visual expression to the idea of the innovative individual looking beyond what others see. The innovative individual also stands alone, though in this case another much like him is about to arrive. The individualist, understood as the creative individual we have described throughout our account of this novel, also stands alone and looks at the world from a perspective few others see. Such a person is not encumbered by pre-existing institutional structures, just as "pinnacles, crowns, and spires" do not obscure Roark's vision. And we need not think of individualism only in "big picture" terms either, for we face "pinnacles, crowns, and spires" virtually every time we face an alternative or make a choice. The final scene, therefore, is an image of individualism. But of course, if individualism really is central to Americanism, then *The Fountainhead* is the quintessential American novel.

Notes and References

1. Historical Context

1. Excerpted from *Compton's Interactive Encyclopedia.*

2. Rand was often opposed by, and opposed to, so-called liberals and conservatives alike. For a sample of some of her views on liberals and conservatives see *Capitalism: The Unknown Idea* (New York: Signet Books, 1967), 173–91.

3. Ayn Rand, "The Roots of War," in *Capitalism: The Unknown Idea* (New York:, Signet Books, 1967), 35–43.

4. According to Stephen Cox, "The Literary Achievement of *The Fountainhead*," in *The Fountainhead: A Fiftieth Anniversary Celebration* (Poughkeepsie, N.Y.: Institute for Objectivist Studies, 1993), 8.

5. Quoted in Nora Ephron, "A Strange Kind of Simplicity," *New York Times Book Review* (5 May 1968).

6. Material for this section is taken from Barbara Branden, *The Passion of Ayn Rand* (New York: Doubleday & Co., 1986), the best biography of Rand available.

7. Written by Maurice Champagne and published in 1914. See Barbara Branden, *The Passion of Ayn Rand* (New York: Doubleday & Co., 1986), 12ff.

8. The most complete published account of her education is contained in C. M. Sciabarra, *Ayn Rand: The Russian Radical* (University Park: Pennsylvania State University Press, 1995), especially chapters 2 and 3.

9. Whittaker Chambers, "Big Sister Is Watching You," *National Review* (28 December 1957): 596.

10. Most notably in Sciabarra, *Ayn Rand.*

2. The Importance of the Work

1. J. Hector St. John de Crevecoeur, 1782, quoted in Michael Novak, *The Spirit of Democratic Capitalism* (New York: Simon and Schuster, 1982), 147.

2. Dean Alfange, "The American Creed."

3. Critical Reception

1. Lorine Pruette, "Battle against Evil," *New York Times Book Review* (16 May 1943): 7.

2. Diana Trilling, "Fiction in Review," *Nation* (12 June 1943): 843.

3. N. L. Rothman, *Saturday Review* (29 May 1943): 30–31.

4. Nora Ephron, "A Strange Kind of Simplicity" 8.

5. See, for example, *The Fountainhead: A Fiftieth Anniversary Celebration* (Poughkeepsie, N.Y.: Institute for Objectivist Studies, 1993).

6. *New York Times Book Review* (6 October 1996): 57.

7. Barbara Grizzuti Harrison, "Psyching Out Ayn Rand," *Ms.* (September 1978): 24–34.

8. Ibid., 30.

9. Robert L. White, "Ayn Rand: Hipster on the Right," *New University Thought* (Autumn 1962): 57–72.

10. Stephen Cox, "The Literary Achievement of *The Fountainhead*," in *The Fountainhead: A Fiftieth Anniversary Celebration*, 8.

11. Ibid., 14.

12. Mimi R. Gladstein, *The Ayn Rand Companion* (Westport Conn.: Greenwood Press, 1984), 36. See also Ronald E. Merrill, *The Ideas of Ayn Rand* (Chicago: Open Court, 1991), 45.

13. Cf., for example, "About a Woman President," in Leonard Peikoff, ed., *The Voice of Reason* (New York: New American Library, 1988).

14. Mimi Gladstein, "Ayn Rand and Feminism: An Unlikely Alliance," *College English* 39.6 (February 1978): 680–85.

15. James T. Baker, *Ayn Rand* (Boston: Twayne Publishers, 1987), 116; Merrill, *The Ideas of Ayn Rand*, 69–71.

16. Mimi Reisel Gladstein and Chris Matthew Sciabarra, eds., *Feminist Interpretation of Ayn Rand* (University Park: Pennsylvania State University Press, 1998).

17. Brownmiller, excerpted in Mimi Reisel Gladstein and Chris Matthew Sciabarra, eds., *Feminist Interpretation of Ayn Rand* (University Park: Pennsylvania State University Press, 1998); Ulrike Heider, *Anarchism: Left, Right, and Green*, trans. Danny Lewis and Ulrike Bode (San Francisco: City Lights Books, 1994), 106–7.

18. C. M. Sciabarra, *Ayn Rand: The Russian Radical*, (University Park: Pennsylvania State University Press, 1995). See also John W. Robbins, *Answer to Ayn Rand: A Critique of the Philosophy of Objectivism*. (Washington, D.C.: Mt. Vernon Publishing Co., 1974), 46–49, 82–83.

19. Merrill, *The Ideas of Ayn Rand,* 157. Kelley's views are contained in *Feminist Interpretation of Ayn Rand.*

20. Estelle C. Jelinek, "Anais Nin: A Critical Evaluation," in *Feminist Criticism: Essays on Theory, Poetry, and Prose,* ed. Cheryl L. Brown and Karen Olson (Metuchen, N.J.: The Scarecrow Press, Inc., 1978).

21. Albert Ellis, *Is Objectivism a Religion?* (New York: Lyle Stuart, 1968).

22. Jerone Tuccille, *It Usually Begins with Ayn Rand* (New York: Stein and Day, 1972).

23. Eric Mack, "The Fundamental Moral Elements of Rand's Theory of Rights," in Douglas J. Den Uyl and Douglas Rasmussen, eds., *The Philosophic Thought of Ayn Rand* (Urbana: University of Illinois Press, 1984), 122–61.

24. The bibliography provides a listing of some of the relevant works of these individuals.

25. Cf. Leonard Peikoff, *Objectivism: The Philosophy of Ayn Rand* (New York: Dutton, 1991), 198–205.

4. The Philosophical Novel

1. Rand herself says this: "In a certain sense, every novelist is a philosopher, because one cannot present a picture of human existence without a philosophical framework." Preface to *For the New Intellectual* (New York: Signet Books, 1961).

2. See, for example, Moler's discussion of *Pride and Prejudice* in Twayne's Masterworks series.

3. Rand did not meet Frank Lloyd Wright until after the publication of *The Fountainhead,* though she tried to do so. The two did become friends, and he designed her home.

4. Ayn Rand, introduction to *The Virtue of Selfishness* (New York: Signet Books, 1964), vii.

5. In a letter to Isabel Paterson dated 26 July 1945, Rand says: "[I]t is so much easier for me to say it in fiction form, because I am primarily a fiction writer. That's my one real love in life. I have to retrain myself to a nonfiction viewpoint and tone." *Letters of Ayn Rand,* Michael S. Berliner, ed. (New York: Dutton, 1995), 179.

6. I am well aware of Rand's antipathy toward Plato, but that antipathy as well as her accuracy of understanding Plato are not at issue here.

7. Roark says, "[T]o sell your soul is the easiest thing in the world. That's what everybody does every hour of his life. If I asked you to keep your soul—would you understand why that's much harder?" (603). See following text for the contrast between how people are and what they can be.

8. *Letters of Ayn Rand*, 99.

9. These are modernized terms. Aristotle, for example, would use the term *self-sufficiency* rather than *independence*.

10. Ayn Rand, *The Romantic Manifesto* (New York: World Publishing Co., 1969), 100, 102; hereafter cited in the text as *RM*.

11. Romanticism was a school of literature in the nineteenth century, and sometimes Rand refers to it this way. As often as not, however, the term refers to a whole approach to art, and this is how we shall use it here. To distinguish between the two, I shall capitalize the school and lowercase the concept.

12. In her essay "What Is Romanticism?" (to which much of this discussion refers), Rand ranks the Romantic authors. I have ignored the ranking here to make the points more general.

6. Dominique

1. Cited in Barbara Branden, *The Passion of Ayn Rand* (Garden City, N.Y.: Doubleday, 1986), 134.

2. *Letters of Ayn Rand*, 341.

3. Merrill also gives Dominique a central place in his interpretation of *The Fountainhead*. Ronald E. Merrill, *The Ideas of Ayn Rand*, 46.

4. See Ronald E. Merrill, *The Ideas of Ayn Rand*, 289; see also Barbara Branden, *The Passion of Ayn Rand*, 300.

5. See also p. 322, where Dominique is pleased Roark has won a battle and is wondering if her worldview is wrong.

6. In *The Passion of Ayn Rand*, Barbara Branden seems to assert that she does (136).

7. *Letters of Ayn Rand*, 92.

8. Ibid., 226.

9. Barbara Branden, *The Passion of Ayn Rand*, 136.

10. *Letters of Ayn Rand*, 229.

7. Sympathy and Judgment

1. Adam Smith, *Theory of Moral Sentiments* (Indianapolis: Liberty Press, 1982), 13, 116.

2. Quoted in John Mullan, *Sentiment and Sociability* (Oxford, England: Clarendon Press, 1988), 143–44; taken from *Sentimental Magazine* (1774) by an anonymous contributor.

3. Ayn Rand, "The Psycho-Epistemology of Art," in *The Romantic Manifesto*, rev. ed. (New York: Signet Books, 1975), 22.

4. Rand later foregoes *egotism* in favor of *egoism.*

5. *Letters of Ayn Rand,* 282; see also 631.

6. Ibid., 138.

7. Ayn Rand, "Philosophy and Sense of Life," in *The Romantic Manifesto,* 25.

8. Rand, "The Psycho-Epistemology of Art," 19.

9. Ibid., 20.

10. "Art and Cognition," in *The Romantic Manifesto,* 47.

11. Rand, "Art and Sense of Life," in *The Romantic Manifesto,* 39.

12. To be fair, the speeches may be quite effective in moving the reader *to* philosophy.

13. Rand, "The Psycho-Epistemology of Art," 22.

8. Individualism

1. Ayn Rand, "The Only Path to Tomorrow," *Reader's Digest* (January 1944): 88–90.

2. Spinoza, *Ethica,* book 4, Proposition 67. The parallels between Spinoza's connection of reason, life, and activity here and Rand's connection are sometimes quite striking. In the proposition to which we have just referred, for example, Spinoza goes on to say: "[A] free man, that is to say, a man who lives according to the dictates of reason alone ... directly desires the good.... [T]hat is to say ... desires to act, to live, and to preserve his being in accordance with the principle of seeking his own profit [*utile*]." (White translation)

3. I do not mean to give the impression that this speech is so neatly categorized. Topics that I have relegated to one section are certainly mentioned in others and vice versa. But the speech does seem to have some topical areas.

4. I assume Rand means that this is the fundamental obligation, not the only one, although the sentence would seem to suggest otherwise. It is legitimate to put the sentence this way, since the speech is about essentials, not derivatives.

9. Conclusion: An American Novel

1. Stephen Cox, "The Literary Achievement of *The Fountainhead*," 7.

2. Ibid., 10.

Bibliography

Primary Sources

Anthem. London: Cassell and Company, 1938. Revised edition, Los Angeles: Pamphleteers, Inc., 1946; Caldwell, Idaho: The Caxton Printers, 1953. Paperback: New York: New American Library, 1946.

Atlas Shrugged. New York: Random House, 1957. Thirty-fifth anniversary edition. Reprint: New York: Dutton, 1992. Paperback: New York: New American Library, 1957.

Capitalism: The Unknown Ideal. New York: New American Library, 1966. Paperback: New York: New American Library, 1967.

The Early Ayn Rand. New York: New American Library, 1984. Edited and annotated by Leonard Peikoff. A selection from her unpublished fiction.

For the New Intellectual. New York: Random House, 1961. Paperback: New York: New American Library, 1961.

The Fountainhead. New York: The Bobbs-Merrill Company, 1943. Afterword by Leonard Peikoff. Twenty-fifth anniversary edition, 1968. Fiftieth anniversary edition, 1993. Paperback: New York: New American Library, 1952.

Introduction to Objectivist Epistemology. New York: New American Library, 1979. Second revised edition, edited by Harry Binswanger and Leonard Peikoff, 1990.

Journals of Ayn Rand. David Harriman, ed. New York: Dutton, 1997.

The Letters of Ayn Rand. Michael S. Berlinger, ed. New York: Dutton, 1995.

The New Left: The Anti-Industrial Revolution. New York: New American Library, 1971.

Night of January 16th. New York: Longmans, Green, 1936. Paperback: New York: World Publishing Co., 1968; reprint, New York: New American Library, 1971.

Philosophy: Who Needs It? Introduction by Leonard Peikoff. New York: The Bobbs-Merrill Company, Inc., 1982.

Bibliography

The Romantic Manifesto. New York: The World Publishing Company, 1969. Paperback: New York: New American Library, 1971. Second revised edition, 1975.

The Virtue of Selfishness. New York: New American Library, 1964.

We the Living. New York: The Macmillan Company, 1936; reprint, London: Cassell, 1937; reprint, New York: Random House, 1959. Paperback: New American Library, 1959.

Newsletters

Rand, Ayn, et al. *Objectivist Newsletter.* Volumes 1–4. New York: The Objectivist, Inc., 1962–1965.

————.*Objectivist.* Volumes 5–10. New York: The Objectivist, Inc., 1966–1971.

Rand, Ayn, and Leonard Peikoff. *Ayn Rand Letter.* Volumes 1–4. New York: The Ayn Rand Letter, Inc., 1971–1976.

Secondary Sources

Books about Ayn Rand

Baker, James T. *Ayn Rand.* Boston: Twayne, 1987.

Binswanger, Harry, ed. *The Ayn Rand Lexicon: Objectivism from A to Z.* Introduction by Leonard Peikoff. New York: New American Library, 1986. A useful compendium of Rand's ideas and their sources in her work.

Branden, Barbara. *The Passion of Ayn Rand.* Garden City, N.Y.: Doubleday, 1986. One of the most complete and informative biographies of Ayn Rand by someone who for many years was close to her.

Branden, Nathaniel. *Judgment Day.* Boston: Houghton Mifflin Company, 1989. Branden's account of his relationship with Ayn Rand.

Branden, Nathaniel, and Barbara Branden. *Who Is Ayn Rand?* New York: Random House, 1962. Includes the first biography sanctioned by Rand.

Cox, Stephen, and David Kelley. *The Fountainhead: A Fiftieth Anniversary Celebration.* Poughkeepsie, N.Y.: Institute for Objectivist Studies, 1993.

Den Uyl, Douglas J., and Douglas Rasmussen, eds. *The Philosophic Thought of Ayn Rand.* Urbana: University of Illinois Press, 1984. A significant academic study of Rand's philosophy.

Ellis, Albert. *Is Objectivism a Religion?* New York: Lyle Stuart, 1968. A critical account of Rand and her philosophy and its psychological impact on her followers.

Erickson, Peter. *The Stance of Atlas.* Portland, Oreg.: Herakles Press, Inc., 1997.

Gladstein, Mimi Reisel. *The Ayn Rand Companion.* Westport, Conn.: Greenwood, 1984. A useful companion source to Rand's works.

———, and Chris Matthew Sciabarra. *Feminist Interpretations of Ayn Rand.* University Park: Pennsylvania State University Press, 1999.

Merrill, Ronald E. *The Ideas of Ayn Rand.* LaSalle, Ill.: Open Court, 1991. A generally sympathetic account of Rand written in a nontechnical way.

O'Neill, William F. *With Charity toward None: An Analysis of Ayn Rand's Philosophy.* Totowa, N.J.: Littlefield, Adams, 1977. A very critical account of Rand's ideas.

Peikoff, Leonard. *Objectivism: The Philosophy of Ayn Rand.* New York: Dutton, 1991. The "official" secondary account of Rand's philosophy by her handpicked intellectual heir.

Robbins, John W. *Answer to Ayn Rand: A Critique of the Philosophy of Objectivism.* Washington, D.C.: Mt. Vernon Publishing Co., 1974.

Sciabarra, Chris M. *Ayn Rand The Russian Radical.* University Park: Pennsylvania Sate University Press, 1995. The only work that sets Rand in a historical context.

Smith, George H. *Atheism, Ayn Rand, and Other Heresies.* Buffalo, N.Y.: Prometheus, 1991.

Torres, Louis, and Michelle Marder Kamhi. *What Art Is: The Esthetic Theory of Ayn Rand.* Chicago: Open Court, forthcoming. A sustained study of Rand's aesthetic philosophy.

Tuccille, Jerome. *It Usually Begins with Ayn Rand.* New York: Stein and Day, 1972. An account of Rand's place within and effect on the Libertarian movement.

Books Based on Rand's Ideas or of Related Interest

Branden, Nathaniel. *The Psychology of Self-Esteem: A New Concept of Man's Psychological Nature.* Los Angeles: Nash, 1969. Rand's philosophical principles applied to psychology. Also the pioneer book of the self-esteem movement.

Gotthelf, Allan, and James G. Lennox, eds. *Philosophical Issues in Aristotle's Biology.* New York: Cambridge University Press, 1987. The topic is Aristotle, but this scholarly treatment by two followers of Rand is important for understanding what may or may not be plausible in the foundations of Rand's ethics.

Bibliography

Hessen, Robert. *In Defense of the Corporation.* Stanford, Calif.: Stanford University, Hoover Institution, 1979. A defense of the nature of corporations as opposed to their practices.

Hospers, John. *Libertarianism: A Political Philosophy for Tomorrow.* Los Angeles: Nash, 1971. A basic explanation of this political ideology. Not directly on Rand but useful nonetheless.

Kelley, David. *The Evidence of the Senses: A Realist Theory of Perception.* Baton Rouge: Louisiana State University Press, 1986. An academic expansion on and defense of Rand's epistemological ideas.

———. *The Art of Reasoning.* New York: W. W. Norton, 1988.

Machan, Tibor. *Human Rights and Human Liberties.* Chicago: Nelson Hall, 1975. A defense of natural rights based on Randian principles. A pioneer work in the academic extension of Randian ideas.

———, ed. *The Libertarian Alternative.* Chicago: Nelson Hall, 1977. A collection of essays, some of which are related to or based on Rand.

Peikoff, Leonard. *The Ominous Parallels: The End of Freedom in America.* New York: Stein & Day, 1982. A work, written under Rand's auspices, about global political trends.

Rasmussen, Douglas B., and Douglas J. Den Uyl. *Liberty and Nature: An Aristotelian Defense of Liberal Order.* LaSalle, Ill.: Open Court, 1991. Provides an Aristotelian defense of classical liberalism. Some Randian themes.

Smith, George H. *Atheism: The Case against God.* Buffalo, N.Y.: Prometheus, 1979. Applies Rand's philosophy to arguments for God's existence.

Selected Articles

Branden, Nathaniel. "Rational Egoism: A Reply to Professor Emmons." *Personalist* 51 (Spring 1970): 196–211. See entry for Emmons.

———. "Rational Egoism: Continued." *Personalist* 51 (Summer 1970): 305–14.

Childs, Roy A. "Objectivism and the State: An Open Letter to Ayn Rand." In *In Liberty against Power: Essays by Roy A. Childs Jr.* Ed. Kennedy Taylor. San Francisco: Fox & Wilkes, 1994. This "letter" (reprinted here from the original 1969 version) was important to the development of libertarian political ideas.

———. "Ayn Rand: 1905–1982." *Inquiry* (26 April 1982).

Cory, Steven. "Rerouting Ayn Rand's *Virtue of Selfishness.*" *Christianity Today* (18 June 1982): 72.

Cox, Stephen. "Ayn Rand: Theory vs. Creative Life." *Journal of Libertarian Studies* 8 (Winter): 19–29.

Deane, Paul. "Ayn Rand's Neurotic Personalities of Our Times." *Revue des Langues Vivants* 36 (1970): 125–29.

Den Uyl, Douglas J. "Ethical Egoism and Gerwirth's PCC." *Personalist* 56 (Autumn 1975): 432–47. An application of Rand's ethical principles to academic ethics.

———— and Douglas B. Rasmussen. "The Philosophical Significance of Ayn Rand." *Modern Age* 27.1 (1983). An accessible summary of why Ayn Rand might be important as a philosopher.

————. "Nozick on the Randian Argument." *Personalist* 59 (April 1978): 184–205.

Emmons, Donald C. "Discussion—Rational Egoism: Random Observations." *Personalist* 52 (Winter 1971): 95–105.

————. "Discussion: Professor Machan's Observations." *Personalist* 53 (Winter 1972): 71–73. This and the previous article, as well as these two issues of the *Personalist*, question the soundness of egoism and were some of the first serious academic discussions of Rand's ethics and her ethical principles.

Evans, M. Stanton. "The Gospel According to Ayn Rand." *National Review* (3 October 1967):. 1059–63. A leading conservative writer looks at Rand.

Fletcher, Max E. "Harriet Martineau and Ayn Rand: Economics in the Guise of Fiction." *American Journal of Economics and Sociology* 35.2 (April 1976): 224.

Gladstein, Mimi Reisel. "Ayn Rand and Feminism: An Unlikely Alliance." *College English* 39 (February 1978): 680–85.

Hospers, John. "Ethical Egoism: Introduction to Nathaniel Branden's Essay." *Personalist* 51 (Spring 1970): 190–95. See the comments in entries on Emmons. Hospers was the main source for introducing Rand's idea into academic philosophy.

————. "Memoir: Conversations with Ayn Rand." Parts 1 and 2. *Liberty* (July 1970): 23–36; (September 1970): 42–52.

Lennox, James G. "Fletcher's Oblique Attack on Ayn Rand's Economics and Ethics." *American Journal of Economics and Sociology* 35.2 (April 1976): 217–24.

Machan, Tibor R. "Ayn Rand: A Contemporary Heretic?" *The Occasional Review* 4 (Winter 1976): 133–49.

————. "Editorial Introduction: The Significance of Ayn Rand." *Reason* (November 1973): 5. This issue of *Reason* is an interesting early collection of essays on Rand by those not necessarily directly associated with her.

Mark, Eric. "How to Derive Ethical Egoism." *Personalist* 52 (Autumn 1971): 735–43. One of the most important essays in the development of scholarly thinking about Rand's ethics.

Bibliography

Nozick, Robert. "On the Randian Argument." *Personalist* 52 (Spring 1971): 282–304. A criticism of Rand's ethics by one of the leading philosophers and writers on Libertarianism.

Rothbard, Murray N. "Memoir: My Break with Branden and the Rand Cult." *Liberty* (September 1989): 27–32. One of the leading free-market economists discusses his relationship with Rand.

Sciabarra, Chris M. "Ayn Rand's Critique of Ideology." *Reason Papers* 14 (Spring 1989): 34–47.

Smith, Kenneth. "Ayn Rand: Objectivism or Existentialism." *Religious Humanism* 4 (Winter 1970): 23–28.

Veatch, Henry B. "Might 'Objectivism' Ever Become Academically Respectable?" *Liberty* (January 1992): 67. One of the leading Aristotelian philosophers discusses the academic prospects of Objectivism.

White, Robert L. "Ayn Rand: Hipster on the Right." *New University Thought* 2 (Autumn 1962): 57–72.

Index

Index

The Author

Douglas J. Den Uyl, professor of philosophy at Bellarmine College, has written extensively in the areas of ethics, political theory, and the history of philosophy. His work *The Philosophic Thought of Ayn Rand,* coauthored and coedited with Douglas Rasmussen, was one of the first extensive academic treatments of Ayn Rand's philosophy.

The Editor

Robert Lecker is professor of English at McGill University in Montreal. He received his Ph.D. from York University. Professor Lecker is the author of numerous critical studies, including *On the Line* (1982), *Robert Kroetch* (1986), *An Other I* (1988), and *Making It Real: The Canonization of English-Canadian Literature* (1995). He is the editor of the critical journal *Essays on Canadian Writing* and of many collections of critical essays, the most recent of which is *Canadian Canons: Essays in Literary Value* (1991). He is the founding and current general editor of Twayne's Masterwork Studies and the editor of the Twayne World Authors Series on Canadian writers. He is also the general editor of G. K. Hall's Critical Essays on World Literature series.